Modernity and the Rise of the Pocket God

Modernity and the Rise of the Pocket God

JONATHAN J. MIZE

RESOURCE *Publications* • Eugene, Oregon

MODERNITY AND THE RISE OF THE POCKET GOD

Copyright © 2021 Jonathan J. Mize. All rights reserved. Except for brief quotations in critical publications or reviews, no part of this book may be reproduced in any manner without prior written permission from the publisher. Write: Permissions, Wipf and Stock Publishers, 199 W. 8th Ave., Suite 3, Eugene, OR 97401.

Resource Publications
An Imprint of Wipf and Stock Publishers
199 W. 8th Ave., Suite 3
Eugene, OR 97401

www.wipfandstock.com

PAPERBACK ISBN: 978-1-6667-0898-1
HARDCOVER ISBN: 978-1-6667-0899-8
EBOOK ISBN: X978-1-6667-0900-1

JULY 9, 2021

To the two most important families in my life—
Mize & Famularo

"We are always on the anvil; by trials God is shaping us for higher things."
—Henry Ward Beecher

Contents

Acknowledgements | ix

Introduction | xi

Part I: Back When God was the World

Chapter 1	Different Minds	3
Chapter 2	Man and God	Separate but One	10
Chapter 3	God's Village	Satan's City	15
Chapter 4	God's Man	21
Chapter 5	God's Theatre	28

Part II: Getting God Back into the World: A Preview

Chapter 6	What to Avoid	43
Chapter 7	What to Aim For	46

Part III: Foundations of a Living Word

Chapter 8	No Spiritual Cushions	51
Chapter 9	No Spiritual Luxury Without *Spiritual* Submission	59
Chapter 10	Life is The Gift	68
Chapter 11	Black and White	77

PART IV: Coming in from the Rain (But Away from the Spirit)

Chapter 12	The Introduction of Cushion	85
Chapter 13	It's All Gray Now	92
Chapter 14	Proverbs and Prosperity: Modern Theological Missteps	102
Chapter 15	Jesus the Life Coach	110
Chapter 16	Machiavelli Was a Christian	115
Chapter 17	Spiritual Procrastination	121
Chapter 18	Spiritual Masturbation	131
Chapter 19	Don't Forget to Worship Your Pastor (and Your Denomination Too!)	137

PART V: Getting off the Couch and into the Spiritual House

Chapter 20	The Forked Path	145
Chapter 21	What Can Be Done?	149

Bibliography | 161

Acknowledgements

MANY THANKS TO JANNIS and Mike Miori. These wonderful folks took me under their wing and shared with me invaluable scripturally rooted wisdom. The Mioris instilled in me the difference between self-righteous, works-based salvation and Righteous, *Christ*-based salvation. Many of the points I make in this book center on this crucial difference. Without Jannis and Mike's wisdom, this book just wouldn't be the same.

Introduction

It is almost unbearably trite to say that today is an age of *instant gratification*. Of course, many phrases and observations become trite for good reason, namely because, well... they're *true*! No doubt, much modern religion is centered on gratification and quick access. God has become a self-help guru, some sort of little figurine to pull out of one's pocket and stroke whimsically while wishing good things out into the "universe."

Today is the age of self-help and "empowerment," and these faux virtues have seeped into every little crevice that one could have ever hoped to keep pristine.

Perhaps no religion has seen such proliferation of self-help and success mantra as Christianity. We need look no further than the phenomenon of the *prosperity gospel*. In 1985, a popular preacher published a book called *Prosperity: The Choice is Yours*, which essentially asserts that God and Jesus are believers' personal hedge fund managers. This book, along with the ascendency of this preacher's ministry, catapulted to the forefront of Christian society what had before been mere undercurrent. The seed of the "prosperity gospel" had been planted many decades earlier, by the likes of Oral Roberts and A.A. Allen. But its culmination in *Prosperity* was an opulently visceral signal of the state of religious society at large.

With all of this showy religious value around us, it's paramount we ask ourselves *what has happened*. Has man grown further from the Lord? Has the modern world come to beguile man? The answer to both questions almost certainly is—*yes*. But it is utterly useless to affirm this conclusion without searching for explanations and solutions.

In this book, we will muse about our modern world, digging for the rotten roots of our maloriented faith. But we won't focus exclusively on the modern. We will also travel back to the *ancient days*, searching for moral and spiritual treasure to carry back to modernity. At the end of it all, we

INTRODUCTION

may just be able to see the modern age's theological flaws more clearly. But we won't stop there; that would be too dreary!

Once we have finished our historical and cultural journey, we will figure out what us modern folks can do to *change things*. We will channel the awesome power of Christ Jesus, the Savior who certainly cannot fit into our tiny little pockets.

PART I

BACK WHEN GOD WAS THE WORLD

CHAPTER 1

Different Minds

Let's start with a commonsense realization—the mental lives of ancient folks were profoundly different than ours. An ancient and seemingly alien society led to just as alien-seeming manners of thought. But it's extremely hard to put our finger on what was so different and "alien" about the ancient mind.

Fortunately for us, there is no shortage of brilliant minds who have pondered on this very question. Not only have these folks meditated on this question, but they have written a great deal about it. The late Polish linguist and anthropologist Jean Gebser is one such great mind. Gebser published his *magnum opus*, *The Ever-Present Origin*, in 1966.

The modern man tends to view his mind as a "blank slate," a fixed tool of his upon which impressions from the "environment" can be made. Alas, such a view limits the boundaries of the mind. Such a view artificially constrains our study of what it means to be a human *in history*. As the saying goes, "people don't live in a vacuum," and man's environment and culture are constantly changing. Our mind is far from an objective and detached entity. It is this dynamic, historically embedded quality of the mind, contra the "blank slate" view, that Gebser endeavored to explain.

In noting the historical *development* of the human mind, Gebser viewed the evolution of human consciousness as a progressive widening of scope. Gebser saw the movement of the mind as a continuous expansion into higher cognitive and social "dimensions." He posited that the very first form of human consciousness was a "zero-dimensional" state of mind which he called "the archaic structure."

In the archaic structure there were *no distinctions* to be made. Everything was melded together as one continuous and gyrating mass. Man's ego was yet to have emerged. In fact, as Gebser himself noted in *The Ever-Present Origin*, it isn't proper to call the archaic structure a form of "consciousness" at all. To call something "conscious" usually implies the capacity of *differentiation*, or the ability to tell rose from tulip and rock from rainfall.

Gebser explains things like so:

> [T]he early period is that period when the soul is still dormant, and its sleep or dormancy may have well been so deep that even though it may have existed (perhaps in a spiritual pre-form), it had not yet attained consciousness.[1]

However, Gebser doesn't stop here. He doesn't dwell on the negative connotations of such an "archaic pre-consciousness." Gebser acknowledges the fact that those who possessed such a mind were often revered as "holy men" by those after them.

Nonetheless, Gebser still sees the "archaic structure" as an underdeveloped and vulnerable state of mind. But there is another way to view things. We can interpret Gebser's theory through a theological lens. It seems commonsensical to imagine that without the ego and without self-consciousness, it was infinitely easier to embrace the *Holy Spirit* that interpenetrates us all. It is a fascinatingly easy comparison to draw between such a proto-consciousness and the mental states of *Adam* and *Eve* in Eden.[2] This is a comparison that I will make great use of—implicitly and explicitly—for many pages to come.

Despite the intrinsic value in contemplating the nature of such a consciousness, the archaic mental structure won't be of too much use for us in the coming pages. In order for us to fully address the nature of the ancient world and its inhabitants' mental worlds, we must have some sort of mental *differentiation*, an ability to distinguish distinct entities. Thankfully, Gebser's work is so comprehensive as to address each and every step along the way, from archaic pre-consciousness to the modern-day mind.

Next in the chain of evolution (or devolution) is what Gebser calls "the magic structure." This is a type of consciousness that most likely arose

---

1. Gebser, *Ever-Present Origin*, 68.

2. I should mention that Gebser himself did entertain this interpretation, although he never expanded much on it.

around 1 million to 500,000 BC with the intentionality associated with the making of *fire*.[3] Though it could have easily arisen far earlier—several *million* years back—with the use of general tools.

Here's what Gebser has to say about the transition to this second form of consciousness:

> The man of the magic structure has been released from his harmony or identity with the whole. With that a first process of consciousness began; it was still completely sleep-like: for the first time not only was man *in* the world, but he began to face the world in its sleep-like outlines. Therewith arose the germ of a need: that of no longer being in the world but of *having* the world. (emphasis original)[4]

Quite abruptly, we are struck again with the analogy of the *fall of man* from the Garden of Eden.

When Adam and Eve were blanketed by the Holy Spirit, communing intimately with Him, there was no true need for differentiation of any sort. Everything was Holy. Then, the serpent tempted with the promise of the grand ability to tell good from evil. With Cain, this seed of differentiation had fully sprouted into a man solely concerned with what he had *within* the world. Cain is in this sense the ultimate emblem of a differentiated consciousness and a hyper-active ego.

It was the initiation of this so-called magic structure of thinking that paved the way for *civilization* as we know it. Today we have more external distinctions than ever. Granted, our manner of distinction is of a special and highly "sophisticated" breed. Back in the days of "magic," man did not concern himself with "cause and effect" as is dictated by modern science. Despite this, in many ways, the "magic man's" mode of consciousness was far closer to the apprehension of reality as it *truly is* than the modern man's will ever be.

Gebser recognized this much. He highlights the great connectivity of mind innate to the "magic man":

> The more man released himself from the whole, becoming "conscious" of himself, the more he began to be an individual, a unity not yet able to recognize the world as a whole, but only the details (or "points") which reach his still sleep-like consciousness and in

---

3. See Smithsonian's "Human Evolution Timeline" at https://humanorigins.si.edu/evidence/human-evolution-timeline-interactive.

4. Gebser, *Ever-Present Origin*, 70.

turn stand for the whole. Hence the magic world is also a world of *pars pro toto*, in which the part can and does stand for the whole. Magic man's reality, his system of associations, are these individual objects, deeds, or events separated from one another like points in the over-all unity.[5]

In contradistinction to today's form of consciousness, the magic consciousness was a more *intuitive*, less partial variety. The possessor of such a consciousness was able to see "singular" acts of God as something much more than this. The "magic person" apprehended the full distribution of the Holy Spirit in all of its beautiful interconnection.

However unfortunate the Biblical parallels of the transition from "ancient" to "magic" consciousness are, we cannot deny the fascinating *physical* transformations that were taking place in tandem with the *spiritual* deformations.

God was working arduously to adapt man into better alignment with his new spiritual predicament. Around 800,000 to 200,000 years ago—shortly after the discovery of *fire* and all its uses—human brains experienced a massive increase in volume.[6]

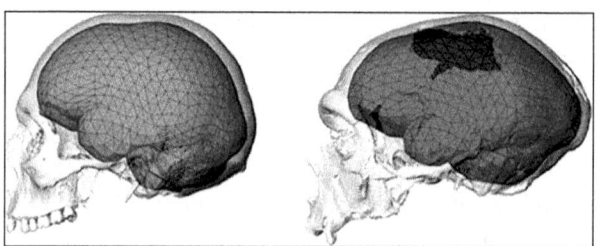

Differences in brain shape between a present-day human (left) and a Neandertal from La Chapelle-aux-Saints (right)[7].

As man's consciousness grew to discern the entities in his environment, new areas of the brain were formed in order to handle the social and physical implications of such newfound distinction. By the time humanity reached the stage of agriculture around 12,000 years ago, the brain and consciousness had fully adapted to deal with the burdens of proliferating

---

5. Gebser, *Ever-Present Origin*, 72.
6. See Neubauer, Hublin, and Gunz's "The evolution of modern human brain shape."
7. Taken from "The evolution of modern human brain shape."

distinction. There was distinction amongst fellow humans, amongst physical entities, and amongst abstract entities such as "currency" and "law."

Let's quickly scale back to "magic consciousness." How did the "magic man" see the world? How did he deal with this new and likely disorienting influx of distinctions and meanings? Gebser gives us a penetrating overview of an answer:

> Man replies to the forces streaming toward him with his own corresponding forces . . . He tries to exorcise her, to guide her; he strives to be independent of her; then he begins to be conscious of his own *will*. Witchcraft and sorcery, totem and taboo, are the natural means by which he seeks to free himself from the transcendent power of nature, by which his soul strives to materialize within him and to become increasingly conscious of itself. . . . Here, in these attempts to free himself from the grip and spell of nature, with which in the beginning he was still fused in unity, magic man begins the struggle for power which has not ceased since; here man becomes the maker. (emphasis original)[8]

Man, recently detached from the Will, is forced to rely upon *his own* will, fumbling about with the forces of his environment.

It is interesting to talk about the concept of "Shamanism" and how those with supposed "magical" (not Christ or Yahweh-centered) powers influenced societies around them. The earliest documented burial of a shaman dates all the way back to the early Upper Paleolithic era of around 30,000 years ago, located in what is present day Czech Republic. In 2008 researchers from the Hebrew University of Jerusalem announced that they had discovered a 12,000-year-old site in Israel that serves as one of the earliest documented shaman burials. The grave site revealed that the elderly woman had been buried with 50 complete tortoise shells, along with various animal body parts, ranging from cow tails and eagle wings to wild boar remains.[9]

There is little wonder why shamans attracted such praise and attention. These people served as their societies' chiefs of nature. The shaman was the prime example of the use of *will power* over the natural world, which back then was quite the recent discovery!

---

8. Gebser, *Ever-Present Origin*. Taken from Mohrhoff's "Evolution of Consciousness According to Jean Gebser," 54.

9. See Harvey and Wallis's *Historical Dictionary of Shamanism*.

PART I : BACK WHEN GOD WAS THE WORLD

Yet, these early benders and shapers of the natural world were far from the most powerful beings that would emerge from the newly differentiated consciousness of man. Anywhere agriculture was practiced on a large scale, shamans fell out of style. Such societies had moved up the "ladder of will," finding more efficient ways to control the world around them. We will see shortly that this new, post-magic age was itself accompanied by a novel form of consciousness.

Ethnologist Leo Frobenius, discussing the magic structure of consciousness, explains the manner of hunting practiced by this sort of man.[10] Before they set out to kill an animal, members of the African Pygmy tribe would draw a picture of the animal in the sand before dawn. Then, at the first strike of sunlight upon the drawing, the hunters would thrust an arrowhead into the neck of the drawing, *symbolizing* a perfect shot. As they went out into the forest to kill the "real" animal, they carried out the destiny of what had been augured by their ritual act. To this ritual, Gebser appends a wonderful explanation:

> The *egolessness* is expressed first of all in the fact that the responsibility for the murder, committed by the group-ego against a part of nature, is attributed to a power already felt to be "standing outside": the sun. It is not the pygmies' arrow that kills, but the first arrow of the sun that falls on the animal, and of which the real arrow is only a symbol. (Nowadays, of course, one would interpret it just the other way around and say: the sun's ray is a symbol of the arrow.) (emphasis original)[11]

This is the perfect description of one of the many semiotic inversions native to the magic structure of consciousness. Linear causality was an alien and completely unfathomable notion. Yet, as much of a beautifully integrated mental life this consciousness afforded, complex and sequentialized social processes such as farming, banking, and politics were utterly *impossible*. This is why we see a sizeable (though imperfect) correlation between the rise of agriculture and the disappearance of shamans and other generalized "magic men."

Gebser goes on to talk about a poignant and bloody encounter between the Spanish and the Aztecs, the ultimate clash between consciousnesses. He speaks of how the Aztec King Moctezuma II sent his city's best sorcerers

---

10. Frobenius, *Kulturgeschichte Afrikas*. Taken from Mohrhoff's "Evolution of Consciousness," 54.

11. Gebser, *Ever-Present Origin*, 77–78.

and magic men out to "cast spells of defense" on the Spanish forces. Not surprisingly, these powers were to no avail against the might of the Spanish military. Gebser says the following:

> The magic-mythical world of the Mexicans could not prevail against the Spaniards; it collapsed the moment it encountered the rational-technological mentality. The materialistic orientation of present-day Europeans will tend to attribute this collapse to the Spaniards' technological superiority, but in actual fact it was the vigor of the Spanish consciousness *vis-à-vis* the weakness of the Mexican that was decisive. It is the basic distinction between the ego-less man, bound to the group and a collective mentality, and the individual securely conscious of his individuality.[12]

On the note of contrast between these two types of consciousness, I'll touch on what Gebser calls "the mythical structure" of consciousness. The progression from magic consciousness to so-called mythical consciousness constitutes a greater capacity of *differentiation* between various "points" in time and space. No longer is the spatio-temporal "manifold" a dynamic and interpenetrating extension of man's consciousness. For the mythical man, this manifold gets flattened out and beaten down. Man is increasingly embedded in the world.

This is where we will begin our investigation of the so-called ancient man. With the rise of agriculture, commerce, and politics came the rise of the city. With the rise of the ancient city came a very unique social milieu.

---

12. Gebser, *Ever-Present Origin*. Taken from Mohrhoff's "Evolution of Consciousness According to Jean Gebser," 56.

CHAPTER 2

Man and God | Separate but One

The "mythical man," son of the "magic man," lost his fathers' ability to see through time, across action and event. The mythical man was primed and ready to *use* the world around him for his own needs.

No matter how unified of an abstraction the "mythical consciousness" seems to appear to us today, there were numerous schisms within it. The days in which the mythical structure ascended were chock-full of cultural change and social schism. In essence, this was "identity politics" on steroids. Myriad tribes, customs and rituals abounded.

Yet, the balance between *difference* and *unity* was struck in a *profoundly different* manner than it has been today. Through all the social subtleties, through all the customs and rituals, the light of the Lord shone far brighter into man's consciousness than it debatably *ever has* for us modern humans. Although there was death, great poverty, and a lack of general "comforts," the Holy Spirit confronted man with a weight and urgency that must have been viscerally palpable. And—perhaps the strangest thing for us modern folks to grasp—the Spirit imbued the ancient man so thoroughly *in virtue* of his plight and in virtue of his material poverty. God in these days was a matter of *life* and *death*, and it was quite difficult indeed for one to escape that fact.

Before I dive deeper into scriptural example, I'll start with a "religiously neutral" example of ancient Egypt. We'll begin by seeing the perilous balance between life and death for the ancient Egyptians.

Counting the infant mortality rates, the overall life expectancy was 19 *years*. In the rare case that someone lived through his/her younger years, this rose to a mere 32 years. The great King Tutankhamun died at 19 years of age. He likely suffered from numerous genetic disorders (from dynastic inbreeding) ranging from Klinefelter syndrome (XXY in males) to Marfan syndrome.[1] Life as an ancient Egyptian—even if you won the lottery of birthright—could be pretty brutal.

To some however, the point just doesn't seem to sink in. There's a certain kind of modern mind that shrugs off the circumstances of those of past generations and attempts to demolish any sort of differences between himself and these people. There is this fundamental insecurity, through which the modern person cannot possibly bear it that their life, as difficult as it subjectively is to them, is far cozier and softer than ancient folks could have ever imagined. This type of person might be tempted to say, "Look, I get that there was disease and death, but weren't their daily routines and emotional lives fundamentally the same as ours?" This is missing the point, plain and simple.

The fundamental emotions of humanity—love, kinship, jealousy and anger—have remained relatively constant. There would be no unified human identity if they hadn't! The point is that what may best be called the "background consciousness" *beneath* these fundamental emotions *has changed*. This much has changed a great deal.

How exactly do we get into the mind of the ancient Egyptian? How do we break free of our modern mental fetters? Interestingly enough, we can start by pondering the state of mind that the modern man possesses when he is alone with and at one with nature. But, before we get to that, I will quickly recap man's recent mental and spiritual trajectory.

As human consciousness has progressed from the "zero-dimensional" mental state of those in Gebser's so-called "archaic structure" of consciousness, all the way to the "mythical structure," man found more and more ways to *divide* and *fracture*. Nonetheless, given the living situations of those possessors of the "mythical structure," the reality of God was omnipresent. The great conquests over evil that the Lord provides were nearly impossible to ignore.

As the centuries wore on and man eagerly found more divisions, fracturing his consciousness even further into a sort of kaleidoscopic disorientation, the new false unities that he experienced with the world—comforts,

---

1. Tyldesley, *Tutankhamen*, 304.

leisures and idle distractions—made it infinitely easier to *drown out* the Divine voice of Yahweh.

Despite this tragic atrophy of the mind, through all of the contemporary noise and flotsam, there are still moments when we can tap into the essence of the "archaic structure" and its intrinsic spiritual unity.

In the article "Phenomenology and Extreme Sports in Natural Landscapes" we catch a glimpse of the interplay between our modern consciousness and the Divine unity. The authors start out by providing a disturbingly accurate picture of the modern day:

> We are now able to delegate many previous activities to robots and other innovative technologies, and even exercise occurs in gyms with monitors measuring our exertion against a screen of outdoor places which are replayed within a bountifully air-conditioned environment. Yet at the same time, we are witnessing higher rates of loneliness, isolation and distress than during any previous time in recorded history. We are spending ever more time in front of a screen which has been linked to poor health and low levels of well-being (Public Health England, 2014).[2]

The article—representing the "secular paradigm" of modern science—neglects to mention the detriments towards *spiritual* health and well-being. But this excerpt illustrates our current mental predicament well enough.

This excerpt introduces a critical dichotomy—that of *control* versus *faith*. This is perhaps the most crucial division that the mythical consciousness spawned, and I believe that it can be used to address nearly *every* extant spiritual issue today. Yes, that's an extremely bold claim; I understand that. But that's just how utterly powerful this tension is.

In the ancient days, man was confronted with the *unforgiving* on a daily basis. What little control the ancient man did wield over his immediate environment was tenuous and shallow. The fickle beast that is nature was omnipresent. If it was raining, one still had to walk the several miles back to his humble dwelling; if the crop season was disastrous, there was little recourse; if one encountered a wild animal on an outing away from the town, one was doomed to perish. It is in this sense that the ancient man was, in many ways, naked.

Here's the crucial question: what replaced the dearth of control in the mind of the ancient man? The answer—*Faith*. Where man couldn't hope

---

2. Brymer and Schweitzer, "Phenomenology and Extreme Sports," 3.

to exert any measure of control over his circumstances, he had little other option but to turn to the Lord.

The discussion of the balance between faith and control is not merely one of "semantics." There were real, living consequences of this fact imprinted upon the ancient mind. In many ways—despite the death, poverty and abundance of uncertainty—the mental life of ancient man was more *romantic* and more *intimate* than the modern man can comprehend. There must have been a deep and poignant relationship with the Lord in these days, as there were few focal points that could divert one's attention from the Almighty for very long. Sure, there were unbelievers and all sorts of evildoers in these days, but those who were devout, I think, were deeply devout.

I've answered the question of why the ancient man was in a unique spiritual position, but I have yet to answer the question of how exactly his consciousness *fit into* his daily life. Yes, the ancient man's mind didn't have as much to focus on or analyze, but how exactly did this *feel* for him? To get a better grasp on this, we will take another look at the article, "Phenomenology and Extreme Sports in Natural Landscapes."

> The central structure of an experience from a phenomenological perspective, is its intentionality, that is, consciousness is directional. For example, within an extreme sports context, Mount Everest presents a good opportunity for understanding intentionality. Climbing is seen, not only as a physical act of moving from the bottom of a mountain to the summit but includes the person's relationship with the mountain and with the Sherpas. Climbing is much more than an activity but is transformed into a meaningful experience and a way of making sense of the world. The Cartesian notions of 'subject' and 'object' are considered coupled and co-constituted in such a way that they cannot conceivably be separated in immediate experience.[3]

We can easily apply this example towards the consciousness of the ancient man and his intimate connection with the Lord.

Back when man's "lifeworld" wasn't separated into myriad quadrants, there was more of a connection with the world.[4] There was less of a boundary between each component and object of the world. When an ancient

---

3. Brymer and Schweitzer, "Phenomenology and Extreme Sports," 4–5.

4. "Lifeworld" is a phrase popularized by the German philosopher Edmund Husserl. One's lifeworld is simply the entirety of one's sensory, emotional, and intellectual experience.

person was tending to their field, they experienced less of a compartmentalized "task" and more of an integrated process, an *engrossing experience*. The psychological phenomenon of "flow"—a mental state in which all distractions largely fade away—was likely a common state of mind for the ancient.[5]

---

5. For an excellent book on "flow," see Csikszent's *Flow*.

CHAPTER 3

God's Village | Satan's City

"Enclosed within his artificial creation, man finds that there is 'no exit'; that he cannot pierce the shell of technology again to find the ancient milieu to which he was adapted for hundreds of thousands of years . . . In our cities there is no more day or night or heat or cold. But there is overpopulation, thralldom to press and television, total absence of purpose. All men are constrained by means external to them to ends equally external."

—Jacques Ellul[1]

In this quote we feel the tension between the fractured modern conscious and the unitary conscious of the ancient. We also see the consciousness of the ancient city-dweller in direct contradistinction to that of the ancient villager. Not so surprisingly, the seeds of the modern fissured consciousness were planted within the walls of the *ancient city*.

I should emphasize that there is nothing innately demonic or degenerate about living in a city or about cities in general. Rather, certain dark and selfish tendencies predispose one to city life, just as city life can imbue the spiritually vulnerable with bad blood.

For the grounding principles behind the city, we need look no further than the writings of the author of the aforementioned quote, Jacques Ellul.

---

1. Ellul, *Technological Society*, 428–29.

PART I : BACK WHEN GOD WAS THE WORLD

Ellul was a marvelously gifted Christian philosopher. He wrote an entire book chronicling the development and institution (*Enoch*) of the city and its impact on the spiritual situation of mankind. Here's a particularly telling excerpt from this book, *The Meaning of the City*:

> For when man is faced with a curse he answers, "I'll take care of my problems." And he puts everything to work to become powerful, to keep the curse from having its effects. He creates the arts and the sciences, he raises an army, he constructs chariots, he builds cities. The spirit of might is a response to the divine curse.[2]

For those acquainted with the scriptural counterpart of this issue, the tale of Cain comes to mind here. After Cain's act of vengeance, the earth and all of mankind fell under a curse, tainted by the spilling of Abel's blood. The fertile face of the earth would no longer bend to Cain's sullied will. Cain set out to construct cities, attempting to erect some sense of security, some sense of personal strength within himself. At the rock bottom of Cain's soul, he was a wanderer, a *fugitive* from the Lord, looking to begin anew.

The story of Cain goes far deeper than this, however. Although it is often stressed that the mark (the promise of protection) God imprinted upon Cain was something he accepted and embraced, there was much psychological strife in Cain over this. As damaged of a heart and mind that Cain was, after he faced his punishment, he was never able to truly *trust* the Lord. In Cain's mind, things were entirely up to *him* and his own will. He fought desperately for the safety and psychological integration that he had forfeited.

Here's something thought-provoking and extremely relevant to our coming story: how exactly did Cain die? Interestingly, the Bible never says that he died *at all*. The soul of Cain is alive and well in the hearts and minds of the modern generation, those who have been cloyingly imbued with the false comforts and safeties of the city.

We can reap great reward from considering the yawning chasm between the souls of *ancient villagers* and those of *ancient and modern city dwellers*. For the former, we need look no further than yet another brilliant quote of Ellul's:

> Prayer is not a discourse. It is a form of life, the life with God. That is why it is not confined to the moment of verbal statement. The latter (verbalization) can only be the secondary expression of the

---

2. Ellul, *Meaning of the City*, 11.

relationship with God, an overflow from the encounter between the living God and the living person.³

The ancient villager embodied this "form of life with God" with great fervor. He lived, ate and breathed the Almighty, drawing his motivation and inspiration from his sense of spiritual purpose. Free from the ambitions that afflicted many city dwellers, the villager desired—first and foremost—to provide abundantly for his family, for his tribe, and for his God. The foundations for a selfless and passionate society were laid outside the city walls, deep within the heart of the ancient village.

Although the chapter title, "God's Village | Satan's City" does have a kernel of truth to it, it would be deceptive to claim that the city *cannot* be used as a force of Good or that it *cannot* evolve into a spiritually beneficial influence. There is profound potential for spiritual integration within the walls of the modern-day city. However, the spiritual philosophy that imbues the modern city should ideally be based on the nature of the *ancient villager's* heart and soul. We must graft the spiritually wedded consciousness of the villager into the inner workings of the modern city. This is how society as a whole will experience a spiritual rejuvenation.

On this note, I have yet another powerful quote from Ellul:

> The city is not just a collection of ramparts with houses, but also it is a spiritual power. [. . .] It is capable of directing and changing a man's spiritual life. It brings its power to bear in him and changes his life.⁴

This is something that is not realized today.

Even amongst the religious, the distinction between the village and the city and its spiritual ramifications are rarely meaningfully discussed. I don't believe that we as a country, the United States of America, have fully recognized the profound importance of the spiritual integrity of the city. We haven't yet recognized what exactly a spiritually integrated network of cities can do for our society. On the topic of the importance of the city, one is reminded of God's attitude towards His cities as seen in Genesis 18:24–32.

---

3. Ellul, *Prayer and Modern Man*, 60.
4. Ellul, *Meaning of the City*, 9.

PART I : BACK WHEN GOD WAS THE WORLD

²⁴ Suppose there are fifty righteous within the city. Will you then sweep away the place and not spare it for the fifty righteous who are in it? ²⁵ Far be it from you to do such a thing, to put the righteous to death with the wicked, so that the righteous fare as the wicked! Far be that from you! Shall not the Judge of all the earth do what is just?" ²⁶ And the Lᴏʀᴅ said, "If I find at Sodom fifty righteous in the city, I will spare the whole place for their sake."

²⁷ Abraham answered and said, "Behold, I have undertaken to speak to the Lord, I who am but dust and ashes. ²⁸ Suppose five of the fifty righteous are lacking. Will you destroy the whole city for lack of five?" And he said, "I will not destroy it if I find forty-five there." ²⁹ Again he spoke to him and said, "Suppose forty are found there." He answered, "For the sake of forty I will not do it." ³⁰ Then he said, "Oh let not the Lord be angry, and I will speak. Suppose thirty are found there." He answered, "I will not do it, if I find thirty there." ³¹ He said, "Behold, I have undertaken to speak to the Lord. Suppose twenty are found there." He answered, "For the sake of twenty I will not destroy it." ³² Then he said, "Oh let not the Lord be angry, and I will speak again but this once. Suppose ten are found there." He answered, "For the sake of ten I will not destroy it."

Sometimes we forget that our God is extremely adamant about seeking out and protecting *spiritual potential*, wherever it may be hiding.

You see, if cities themselves were intrinsically against the Will of God, then He would not care if there happened to be *any* righteous residing within. If He did not care, the very act of inhabiting a city would *negate* one's righteousness in His eyes. Fortunately, this is *far* from the case. The city—though it has myriad vices and maladies—is *not* a spiritual lost cause. We need to sufficiently imbue cities and their citizens with the Blood, so that they may turn towards the *ancient* consciousness, the spiritually unified consciousness of the ancient villager.

Even in the modern age, the bucolic lifestyle that accompanies rural areas has a discernable impact upon faith. According to the Carsey Institute, the percentage of rural folks who say that they attend church weekly is comparatively higher than that of urban and suburban residents.[5] This relationship holds throughout every single American region, from the Northeast to the West. Moreover (also from Carsey's study), the percentage of Americans claiming to have had a "born again" religious experience is sizably higher amongst those in rural areas. Nearly *half* of those living in rural areas claimed to have such an experience, while less than 30 percent of those living in larger cities had! And—just as is the case with church attendance—rural Americans had higher proportions of religious experience across the board, throughout *all* geographical regions of the U.S.

It is just as interesting to note that denizens of rural areas experience more religious cohesion *regardless* of their denomination, just as the study claims below:

---

5. Dillon and Savage, "Values and Religion."

Not surprisingly, given the small-town life of rural residents, the church is a focal point for many, a place where neighbors worship, socialize, and reflect on the state of the country. Rural Americans' denominational preferences tend to vary in distinct ways by region. In the South, for example, most people are Protestant (77 percent), and by and large they are Baptists, mostly Southern Baptists, whose conservative theology has long made a mark on Southern culture and everyday life. Catholics dominate in the East; the Midwest is more mixed, home to a large proportion of Protestants (mostly Lutherans, Methodists, and Baptists) and a sizable number of Catholics; and the West remains the most "unchurched" region in the country.[6]

This excerpt reminds us of the core ingredients comprising the correlation between rural environments and religiosity—communal allegiance and a collective orientation towards Christian values. Even though the idle comforts and distractions of the modern world have wormed their way into today's rural areas, the cultural and social cohesion in place from days past has ensured that the wayward spirits of the city have been unable to invade. When we stack up the routines of rural life next to the hustle and bustle of urban life, we find that there are two core differences between the two. Life in rural areas is accompanied by a sort of "no strings attached" *benevolence* and a certain *intimacy* between people. Life in larger cities comes with a more aloof disposition and a lack of collective intimacy. Let's try and explain these two differences.

NPR has an article on their site, *www.npr.org*, called "Cities — But Not Their Citizens — Really Are Meaner".[7] The article mentions a YouTube video posted by Casey Neistat in which he sets up a hidden camera in downtown NYC, capturing passer-bys' reactions as he stages the theft of his own bike.[8] The piece chronicles a discussion between the media host Jennifer Ludden and writer Will Doig, as they delve into the issue of why people in big cities are so different from their suburban and rural counterparts.

> DOIG: Yes. So city folk basically have this kind of every-man-for-himself reputation of being callous and self-absorbed and indifferent to strangers in need. And this sort of reputation also gets reinforced by, you know, popular culture, Martin Scorsese movies,

---

6. Dillon and Savage, "Values and Religion," 2.
7. Doig and Ludden, "Cities are Meaner."
8. See Neistat's video, "The Ethics of Stealing a Bike," https://www.youtube.com/watch?v=wW6gGyfxn1U

PART I : BACK WHEN GOD WAS THE WORLD

Rick Santorum saying that city people have a different value structure. And it is true, like you said, that urbanites are less likely than people in rural areas to intervene in scenarios involving strangers who need assistance or property being stolen or vandalized.[9]

Mr. Doig hints at the numerous social psychology studies related to the willingness of strangers to assist each other—what we called above "no strings attached benevolence."

The core finding of these studies is that the *more* people there are around to potentially help, the *less* people actually come to someone's assistance. In fact, if the area is sufficiently busy, it is likely that *not a single person* will stop and help a stranger in need. The psychological process behind this is that each given person—seeing the crowd of other strangers around—is extremely likely to *displace the urgency*. In other words, it becomes a sort of "Oh, there's so many people here... one of these *other* people will help her!" kind of rationalizing. For those familiar with economics and social philosophy, the so-called tragedy of the commons is largely parallel to this situation.

However dismal this psychological finding may sound, there is some underlying hope to be found. After Mr. Doig discusses the content and ramifications of the studies, he goes on to mention another extremely important finding:

> But what psychologists have learned is that this doesn't have anything to do with callousness or not caring and more to do with external factors that are more pronounced in urban environments. And the way that they measure that is by doing things like going out with assistance and faking injuries and feigning blindness and dropping pens and things like that and see if anybody...[10]

In other words, it's not always the case that people without the Spirit move to urban cities. It's that the environment of the city is conducive to callous and spiritually detached behavior. This is quite the find! There is hope for our cities after all.

---

9. Doig and Ludden, "Cities are Meaner," lines 20–26.
10. Doig and Ludden, "Cities are Meaner," lines 27–31.

CHAPTER 4

God's Man

> Let no one say when he is tempted, "I am being tempted by God"; for God cannot be tempted by evil, and He Himself does not tempt anyone.
>
> JAMES 1:13

IT IS NO MYSTERY that God is adamant about promises and deals. Some variety of the word "covenant" is found 555 times in the standard works of the Gospel.[1] The Lord Himself refers to the spiritual body of the Gospel as the "everlasting covenant."[2] The covenant—the spiritual, volitional cohesion between *man* and *man* and *God* and *man*—is absolutely paramount to the healthy function of society. Not so surprisingly, it has been utterly neglected by modern society.

Perhaps the most poignant and striking example of a man-to-man covenant in the Bible is that of David and Jonathan. In Samuel 18:3, Jonathan initiated a covenant of friendship with David, because he "loved him as himself." Implicit within a covenant in Biblical times was the fact that the eyes of the Lord observed its formation and expected those involved to hold true to this union.

---

1. See Parker's "Cutting Covenants."
2. This expression occurs sixteen times in the Old Testament and once in the New. See van Bemmelen's, "The Everlasting Covenant" for more detail.

Part I : Back When God was the World

> **18** After David had finished talking with Saul, Jonathan became one in spirit with David, and he loved him as himself. **2** From that day Saul kept David with him and did not let him return home to his family. **3** And Jonathan made a covenant with David because he loved him as himself. **4** Jonathan took off the robe he was wearing and gave it to David, along with his tunic, and even his sword, his bow and his belt.

This covenant was no mere ceremonial or symbolic gesture. This was a pact to mutually dedicate one another's values and empathies. Such a covenant took precedence over other friends and even family, were they to encroach upon its boundaries. In Jonathan's case, his own father, King Saul, came against this covenant in a grave and malicious way, attempting to kill his dear friend David out of blind envy on numerous occasions. After Jonathan discovered his father's malicious intent towards David, he stormed out and refused to eat at the New Moon feast the following day. The day after the feast, he had an emotional meet-up with David.[3]

> **41** After the boy had gone, David got up from the south side of the stone and bowed down before Jonathan three times, with his face to the ground. Then they kissed each other and wept together—but David wept the most.
>
> **42** Jonathan said to David, "Go in peace, for we have sworn friendship with each other in the name of the Lord, saying, 'The Lord is witness between you and me, and between your descendants and my descendants forever.'" Then David left, and Jonathan went back to the town.[b]

This is one of the most impactful examples of man-to-man covenant found anywhere, and its spiritual and social ramifications are far-reaching.

It is a sad fact that the modern Western world has *nothing* resembling this kind of covenant. The closest we get to a covenant is sharing relationship secrets or "road tripping" together. And it seems that this lack of covenant holds true *regardless* of whether one lives in a city or in a small town.

In addition to the gravity of the covenant, we have the relationship between the plans of mere man and the Plan that God provides. Proverbs

---

3. 1 Samuel 20 NIV.

19:21 states, "Many are the plans in the mind of a man, / but it is the purpose of the Lord that will stand."[4] We see a direct relationship between this verse and the forms of consciousness we saw recently. As man's consciousness has progressed throughout society, there has been a cognitive and perceptual fracturing or fissuring. This fissuring has made it easier for the modern man to pursue his *own* plan and shut out His purpose. Pondering on the nature of God and the Spirit, we can see how such a fractured conscious is incompatible with full spiritual integration.

In philosophical language (as opposed to scriptural language), God is the Ultimate Identity of reality. Our Lord is a unified and coherent Being.[5] In order for us to commune with Him, we must ourselves be coherent and unified on at least some level. John 4:24 gives us a perfect perspective on this: "God is spirit, and those who worship him must worship in spirit and truth."[6] Today, sadly, not only do we have a surging number of ADHD diagnoses, but we have an ever-increasing infestation of ADHD *of the spirit*. These two maladies often go hand in hand.

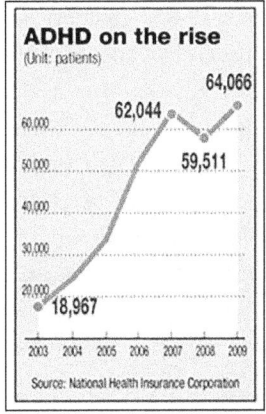

Imagine a chart stretching all the way back to 2,000BC, charting the statistics of *spiritual* ADHD. We would see a very similar looking trend.

What exactly do I mean by "ADHD of the spirit?" Isn't this just a cute but unnecessary nickname? No, not exactly. Contemplating what usually

---

4. ESV.

5. See Mize and Geilenberg, "Panentheism: A Category-Theoretic Approach" for my personal take on the more philosophical, mathematical view of God.

6. ESV.

PART I : BACK WHEN GOD WAS THE WORLD

accompanies the modern diagnosis of "ADHD"—trouble focusing, hyperactivity, impulsiveness—the parallels between this and the deeper issues of the spirit are clear. For purposes of clarification, we can view the physical variety of ADHD as a disease of the *soul* (the mind and emotions), while viewing the spiritual variety as a disease of the *spirit* (the connection to God; the source of human meaning). In drawing a line between "soul" and "spirit" I don't intend to bind myself to any particular theology; it is merely a tool.

Modern cities have been afflicted especially hard with these tandem diseases—ADHD of the soul *and* ADHD of the spirit. It will be telling to examine the relationship between the two varieties. When we take a closer look, we will see how they needn't always go hand in hand.

In ancient cities, ADHD of the *spirit* was the most common variety, perhaps even exclusively so. The environment of the ancient city—though it could be sensually stimulating and distracting from more contemplative forms of activity—did not usually fully fracture the ancient's conscious so as to disorient his soul. How is it then that the ancient city came to be so *spiritually* disoriented? In short, spiritual ADHD forms slowly, gently nudging its way into society until its effects cannot be ignored.

Just as traditional ADHD makes it extremely challenging to learn in the classroom, ADHD of the spirit makes it extremely hard to absorb the wisdom and insight of the Lord. This spiritual disorder can give its owner false confidence in having learned and taken to heart the most important principles of the Lord, while his never having *truly heard* them. Such spiritual inattention calls to mind Jesus's explanation of his ministerial approach in Matthew 13:13: "This is why I speak to them in parables: 'Though seeing, they do not see; though hearing, they do not hear or understand. . .'" It is possible for one with mere ADHD of the soul to imbibe the Lord's wisdom, yet it is essentially impossible for one with severe ADHD of the *spirit* to take anything more than a superficial helping of His Goodness.

When we look at God's ideal soul and spirit, we see a *placid* and *directed* consciousness and spirit. We see eager attention and devotion towards the Lord and His word. It was far easier for the ancient villager to attain a tranquil and intent consciousness. His environment was highly conducive to such states of mind.

In terms of the ancient city-goers, there is a very broad range of spiritual and soulful possibilities. There's the possibility that an ancient person traveled to the city after already having an inattentive and restless soul.

However, given that the life of a villager in these times did not usually encourage atrophy of the soul, this is not a very likely scenario. There's also the possibility that one moved to the city with a perfectly healthy soul, but, after having been ingratiated into the city's disorienting, fast-pace lifestyle, ended up with an ailing one. Given the contrast between the ancient village and the ancient city, this seems to be the most likely scenario.

Yet another possibility is that one moved to the city, soul inattentive and restless, yet was magically "healed" by the new lifestyle, finding rejuvenation of the soul. If I were to add in all the possibilities including the maladies of the *spirit*, things would become unnecessarily complicated.

Let's take a look at a highly interesting scenario from the above possibilities. Let's say we have an ancient villager, call him Aaron. Suppose that before Aaron decided to come to the city, he had both an inattentive soul *and* spirit. Aaron was very troubled. However, after he ingratiated himself into the ways of the ancient metropolis, Aaron experienced a newfound direction of *soul*. Aaron was called to become a great politician and landowner. (I speak generally here, as in some ancient societies such a movement of "class" was unattainable.) Given the lack of spiritual direction in Aaron's decisions, he was unable to scrape away the grime left by years of inattention off of his spirit. Aaron was transformed into a ruthless, steely-eyed statesman.

What's the significance of this story? This is what's known in the modern day as a "success story." This is the kind of thing that the modern man writes heavy books on and makes dramatic films about. Of course, the writers conveniently neglect to mention the role of the *spirit*; that's less than an afterthought.

Aaron's story is the modern-day "hit," but what is *God's* ideal success story?

Let's introduce another ancient man named Gabriel. Gabriel was a big shot in the city he was in, serving in office and accumulating quite the sum of money. Given Gabriel's wild success, his soul was steadfastly focused on the here and now; he had no inattention or restlessness in that regard. However, Gabriel's political life gradually gnawed away at his spirit, until there was little left but an undersized, shaking little lump of a connection with God. Miraculously, one day, the wisdom of James 1:9–10 hit him squarely in the face.

The Lord told him something like this, "Gabriel, the brother in humble circumstances should exult in his high position. The one who is rich should exult in his low position, because he will pass away like a flower of the field." Being sufficiently touched by this Wisdom, Gabriel decided to give everything up. He renounced all of his positions in the city and moved to a farming village by the river.

This is the perfect inversion of the above story of Aaron. Unlike Aaron, Gabriel—though he lost his status and his material possessions—attained true spiritual balance and genuine intimacy with the Lord. Unfortunately, this story isn't as "sexy." The pop culture of today couldn't care less about it!

> Jeremiah 6:16
> New International Version
>
> **16** This is what the Lord says:
>
>> "Stand at the crossroads and look;
>>   ask for the ancient paths,
>> ask where the good way is, and walk in it,
>>   and you will find rest for your souls.
>>   But you said, 'We will not walk in it.'

More than ever, we need to heed these words. We need to look back to the "ancient paths" and seek the wisdom of our ancestors in the Lord. Unfortunately, in today's social, spiritual and political climate, such an urging may be unfairly targeted as "new age" or "alternative," as paradoxical as such classifications no doubt are.

Many modern churches focus exclusively on the present day. They of course utilize scripture, but they neglect to truly examine (much less *disseminate*) the nuggets of spiritual wisdom that can be found in the mind of the ancient man.

It should be clear by now that God's ideal person possesses a balanced, calm spirit and soul. In order for us to receive more than intermittent tidbits of Divine wisdom and guidance, we need at least some degree of coherence and unity within ourselves. This much is paramount.

Moreover, we have seen how the man of yore was not only able to receive the spiritual gifts for himself but was also adept at *sharing* these great gifts with his brothers and sisters. In common sense terms, how can we expect to form spiritual covenants with our fellow citizens if we cannot so much as integrate our *own* soul and spirit?

CHAPTER 5

God's Theatre

With all I've said about God's children and their motivations and interactions, I have yet to deeply discuss society *as a whole*. We've seen the effects that the village and the city had upon the consciousness of man, but we haven't yet seen the societal interplay between those affected. How exactly do people's consciousnesses impact the society they live in?

Culture and politics intersect to begin with, but only once we begin to look at their intersections through a more *spiritually* informed lens can we begin to glean some useful information.

Romans 12:2 gives us an excellent waypoint for our investigations: "Do not be conformed to this world, but be transformed by the renewal of your mind, that by testing you may discern what is the will of God, what is good and acceptable and perfect."[1] Not only this, but we also have the wisdom of Titus 2:1–15:

> But as for you, teach what accords with sound doctrine. Older men are to be sober-minded, dignified, self-controlled, sound in faith, in love, and in steadfastness. Older women likewise are to be reverent in behavior, not slanderers or slaves to much wine. They are to teach what is good, and so train the young women to love their husbands and children, to be self-controlled, pure, working at home, kind, and submissive to their own husbands, that the word of God may not be reviled.[2]

1. ESV.
2. ESV.

On one hand we have the call to dig beneath one's cultural and societal surroundings and imbed one's mind deeply in the Lord. On the other hand we have the injunction to *allow* the older generations to provide us with their wisdom, guidance and reassurance under God.

Such a contrast reminds us of politics and ideology. In America, we have two core bodies of thought—"progressivism" and "conservativism." Each of these sides proposes a very different answer to the issue of heeding wisdom of years past. In the modern age, this schism reigns supreme.

It is interesting to examine the ideal of Titus 2:1–15 in terms of the modern ideology of *political conservativism* and all that it stands for. Perhaps in virtue of its name only, political conservatism is often lambasted for being an overly "traditional" or "backwards" ideology, something that prizes rigid moralism over emotional and social flexibility. Both descriptors—*traditional* and *backwards*—are improper on multiple accounts.

In regard to the first adjective, it would be a sorry mistake to claim that political conservatism advocates a sort of blind allegiance to tradition. Conservativism is not a relative, looking glass ideology. It is based upon timeless principles of liberty, temperance and reverence, and it does not advocate anything that is unnecessarily rigid or tied to mere cultural circumstance.

Addressing the second adjective, something is only "backwards" if the current social circumstances *no longer require* the principles in question. Given the atemporality of the principles that America was founded upon, this much is a logical and moral impossibility.

As deeply rooted and socially sound as the principles of American conservativism are, we still have a lot to improve upon as believers and citizens of the United States. We have a lot to learn from our ancient brothers and sisters.

We have many conservatives who neglect to imbibe the advice and wisdom of their older family and older friends, just as we no doubt have many believers who are mired in idolatry of tradition and superfluous custom. Regarding these loose ends, Colossians 2:8 is a perfect place to start:

> See to it that no one takes you captive by philosophy and empty deceit, according to *human tradition*, according to the *elemental spirits of the world*, and not according to Christ. For in him the whole fullness of deity dwells bodily, and you have been filled in him, who is the head of all rule and authority. In him also you were circumcised with a circumcision made without hands, by putting off the body of the flesh, by the circumcision of Christ,

PART I : BACK WHEN GOD WAS THE WORLD

> having been buried with him in baptism, in which you were also raised with him through faith in the powerful working of God, who raised him from the dead. (emphasis added)³

God's ideal soul and spirit are integrated and coherent wholes. We've already seen this much. By implication, God's ideal *society* is an integrated and coherent intermeshing of souls and spirits.

In this light, anything that binds one to human tradition or elemental spirits is a source that fractures one's spirit, sullying the unity thereof. The entire division of the political landscape into "Republican" and "Democrat" is a paradigmatic instance of such fissuring of the spirit. If we are to transcend our cultural and traditional limitations and move into the body of Christ in unity, we must eventually discard these divisions.

Despite all our modern chaos, it is tempting to think that we may be more culturally unified than folks were in the ancient days. Yet, this assumption glosses over the various forms of cultural cohesion that thrived in the ancient times. Although it is true that the politics of many ancient societies were no greater (and, often, far worse) than our current systems, we must remember that what the ancient days lacked in overt political capacity they made up for tenfold in their wealth of social, cultural and spiritual *cohesion*.

I should briefly mention what I mean by "ancient." The term is no doubt a rather sloppy and broad word. To many people this word may conjure up images of great pharaohs, tabernacles and mud dwellings, juxtaposed with majestically stone-worked buildings and churches. These visions actually make up only an extremely small portion of what I mean by the "ancient world" and "ancient society."

For our usage, I will consider the descriptor "ancient" as that which took place *before* the fifteenth- and sixteenth-century "Renaissance." In this sense I will talk abstractly about the different material and cultural conditions of the "ancient" man. I take ancient to mean simply "pre-Renaissance," so that we can strip away all negative connotations of the word and dig into the core of the ancient spirit.

Having ironed this out, I will talk about the various forms of cultural and social cohesion that abounded back in ancient times.

What we can glean from our previous discussions of consciousness and society is that, once the basic mode of interaction and cultural value is

3. ESV.

altered, the very fabric of political and economic exchange begins to shift, molding into a beautifully interconnected web of soul and (ideally) spirit.

On the topic of society and principles of exchange, Economics professor Elinor Ostrom, in her book *Governing the Commons: The Evolution of Institutions of Collective Action* (1990), shows how close-knit communities can overcome various problems of social coordination. Ostrom provides numerous counterexamples to the infamous "tragedy of the commons." The tragedy of the commons is a paradox of human will where that which is collectively owned tends to *deteriorate* for lack of collective upkeep. The tragedy of the commons represents a strict departure from Christly wisdom. It signals a lack of Christly covenant and collective commitment.

Near the beginning of Ostrom's book she has a section entitled "Communal Tenure in High Mountain Meadows and Forests" where discusses the communal upkeep and governance of the mountain meadows of Törbel, Switzerland.

Taken from https://www.gruppenhaus.ch/en/house/holiday_house/toerbel/126. Törbel is essentially the definition of an idyllic and peaceful village. One can imagine that it would be easier to incline one's ear to the Lord in such an environment.

Törbel still exists as a municipality in modern-day Switzerland, having withstood the test of time for many centuries. Ostrom tells us that written legal documents dating back to the year 1224 give information on the kinds of land tenure and transfer that occurred in Törbel. Several centuries later, in 1483, the residents of Törbel signed a formal agreement establishing an association to achieve a more integrated and efficient method of commons regulation. In essence, this Swiss village established a *covenant* amongst all citizens. Not too long after the relevant documentation was drafted, in 1507, boundaries of the *communally owned* lands were established.

Such communally organized undertakings no doubt occurred far earlier than the early sixteenth century. In the case of Törbel, we have been blessed with long-lasting and interpretable documents and remains.

Ostrom goes on to tell us about the village's way of life:

> Access to well-defined common property was strictly limited to citizens, who were specifically extended communal rights. As far as the summer grazing grounds were concerned, regulations written in 1517 stated that "no citizen could send more cows to the alp than he could feed during the winter" (Netting 1976, p. 139). That regulation, which Netting [a historian] reports to be still enforced, imposed substantial fines for any attempt by villagers to appropriate a larger share of grazing rights. Adherence to this "wintering" rule was administered by a local official (*Gewalthaber*) who was authorized to levy fines on those who exceeded their quotas and to keep one-half of the fines for himself.[4]

This sort of communally enforced commitment calls to mind the wisdom of Paul found in Ephesians 4:1–6:

Unity and Maturity in the Body of Christ

4 As a prisoner for the Lord, then, I urge you to live a life worthy of the calling you have received. **2** Be completely humble and gentle; be patient, bearing with one another in love. **3** Make every effort to keep the unity of the Spirit through the bond of peace. **4** There is one body and one Spirit, just as you were called to one hope when you were called; **5** one Lord, one faith, one baptism; **6** one God and Father of all, who is over all and through all and in all.

Now is a wonderful time to revisit the theme of *unity* of the Spirit and of man's constituent spirits.

When we connect this imperative of unity and coherence to the social milieu of the medieval village of Törbel, we can see the great spiritual force that is the village, and if we squint hard enough, the *city* as well.

---

4. Ostrom, *Governing the Commons*, 62.

Here's a sad fact—the modern city and "suburbia" are no more conducive to spiritual unity than a clear sky is conducive to producing a rejuvenating rain. No, I don't mean to say that communal organization is the most optimal method of economic construction *currently* available. Neither do I claim that such an economic system would single handedly draw folks closer to God. I concede—we need *far more* than mere man-made political organization to do this.

The point I'm making is this—if *all citizens* of any given country, city or society were imbued fully with the Spirit and were endowed with unified consciousness, we would likely see a societal arrangement much like the communalism seen in medieval Törbel. We would see a Spiritual communalism in which each and every citizen treated every communal decision as a *covenant* under the eyes of the Lord.

If each and every person were imbued by the Spirit, there would be no need for domineering structures of government. All conceivable man-made systems and ideologies—capitalism, socialism, communism, anarchism, traditionalism, and yes, *even communalism itself*—would fade away, replaced by Divine reverence and insight.

Just to reiterate, I am absolutely not saying that the United States government should immediately or forcefully transition to a communal mode of economic organization. Such a move would be horribly uninformed, and the crucial component would be missing, the only component that even matters—God, His Son and the Holy Spirit.

The point of all this "communalism" talk is that we still have a spiritual, social *goal* towards which we should all strive.

In a communalist society, we see the fusion of the three core components of a Holy society—(1) a unity and dedication of consciousness under Christ, (2) a respect for man-to-man covenant under the Lord, and (3) the lack of unrestrained ambition of the soul that one sees so often in the modern city.

Any and all ties of communalism to "anarchism" and "libertarian socialism" are null and void in this case.[5] In such a *Christly* communal society, there would not necessarily even be norms or barriers against becoming wealthy. As long as there was man-to-man covenant under the

---

5. It is an unfortunate fact that the term "communalism" has been associated with the various subversive and borderline demonic ideologies of man. Murray Bookchin, a self-proclaimed "libertarian socialist," popularized the term in his voluminous writings. But the concept behind the term has been alive since Biblical days.

Lord and the wealth did not distract its owner from his dedication to the Lord, there would be no issue.

Such a "Christly communal" society would be completely and utterly different from any "ism" yet proposed by man. Such a society would instead be proposed by *the principles of the Lord*.

Let's take a bit of a turn. I'd like to see how all of this rather abstract talk relates to something more concrete. Let's pick out a modern, Christian movement—the so-called *prosperity gospel*. How does the talk of a "communal" society in Christ address this modern phenomenon?

I will shy away from naming names or pronouncing judgements. Instead, I will focus on the *content* of the prosperity gospel message. We'll begin by taking a look at the brilliantly informative *Blessed: A History of the American Prosperity Gospel* (2018) by Kate Bowler. Bowler's work is an excellent example of a balanced, sociologically informed exposition of the prosperity gospel.

> From the beginning, Christians sought to access supernatural power for their daily lives, and the chief way they tried to do so was through prayer: requests from helpless humans to an omnipotent God who heard these pleas and might—or might not—answer them as desired by the petitioners. [. . .] *Finding this method and its subordination of the self to be irksome and ineffective* Christians often sought to *compel the supernatural to produce their desired results.* [. . .] *Magic* took two main forms, material and mental. *Material magic* employed "spells, symbols, artifacts, and actions" to effect change, whereas *mental magic* made use of "vision, reverie, meditation, and affirmative prayer." (emphasis added)[6]

Here we see something quite profound—there is a sense in which the prosperity gospel is a malorientation of the will. It can be seen as a turning against the Plan of the Will, towards the plans of their mere will.

The mantra of the prosperity gospel bears uncanny resemblance to Jean Gebser's characterization of the "the magic structure of consciousness" I mentioned a few chapters ago.[7] In other words, there is a sense in which the "prosperity gospel" way of thinking resembles that of *prehistoric* humans. To those with the "magic structure" wired into their brains, the world is very sympathetic to incantations and "manifestations."

---

6. Bowler, *Blessed* (PhD thesis version), 28.
7. Gebser, *Ever-Present Origin*.

Once man fell down from the "archaic structure" of unified consciousness found in Adam and Eve—once the gates were closed and the scarily powerful cherubim were installed—man was confronted with the yawning chasm between his own will and the Will of the Almighty. The direct effects of such a psychological confrontation can be found in Cain and his precious Enoch.

In Bowler's excerpt about the foundations of the prosperity gospel, we see an eerie parallel between the fixation of the soul upon *material* prosperity and the substitution of *spiritual unity* under the Lord for the *false unity* of material comfort. This is redolent of the following excerpt from Gebser's *Ever-Present Origin*:

> The more man released himself from the whole, becoming "conscious" of himself, the more he began to be an individual, a unity not yet able to recognize the world as a whole, but only the details (or "points") which reach his still sleep-like consciousness and in turn stand for the whole. Hence the magic world is also a world of *pars pro toto*, in which the part can and does stand for the whole. Magic man's reality, his system of associations, are these individual objects, deeds, or events separated from one another like points in the over-all unity.[8]

In the teachings and culture of the prosperity gospel, we see this *pars pro toto* manifest itself as the obsessive worship of money. The earthly greenback grows to replace all the *immaterial* Grace and Purpose of the Lord. Salvation is no longer seen as a spiritual treasure, but as a physical treasure. Folks under this spell look to satiety and safety for spiritual satisfaction.

This "prosperity gospel" way of thought is a spiritual sleight of hand, plain and simple. It is an unfortunate result of the modern, fractured conscious of man.

Of course, there are numerous ways in which proponents of the prosperity gospel can retaliate against these claims. They can say that their teachings simply urge one to have more faith in the Lord. They can (and do) argue persuasively that money is just another form of "safety" or "blessing," regardless of whether it can be sanctioned by both man and God. To the acknowledgement of these fellow believers, these folks don't make too bad of an argument. It is completely possible that their hearts are genuinely after the Lord, and I cannot judge them in that regard. Yet, as far as their

---

8. Gebser, *Ever-Present Origin*. Taken from Mohrhoff's "Evolution of Consciousness According to Jean Gebser," 54.

own "school" of theology and interpretation of Scripture go, we can say more than a few words in return.

I can sum up my argument against the "prosperity" style of thinking like so: if you fail to make a personal covenant with the Lord that *all of* the material possessions you have received are to be used first and foremost for His Will, then you are engaging in *idolatry*.

Simply speaking, there is *no* restriction that idolatry be something *external* to one's self. Idolatry, especially in modern times, can invade one's heart and embed itself deeply within the soul, siphoning off the Spirit and transducing its message into warped and egotistical fantasy. In the case of prosperity theology, the idol isn't necessarily the physical money. The idol is the personal will, the self-image and the self-esteem. When these elements are mixed without temperance, *self-righteousness* is often the resulting cocktail.

The Parable of the Pharisee and the Tax Collector

[9] To some who were confident of their own righteousness and looked down on everyone else, Jesus told this parable: [10] "Two men went up to the temple to pray, one a Pharisee and the other a tax collector. [11] The Pharisee stood by himself and prayed: 'God, I thank you that I am not like other people—robbers, evildoers, adulterers—or even like this tax collector. [12] I fast twice a week and give a tenth of all I get.'

[13] "But the tax collector stood at a distance. He would not even look up to heaven, but beat his breast and said, 'God, have mercy on me, a sinner.'

[14] "I tell you that this man, rather than the other, went home justified before God. For all those who exalt themselves will be humbled, and those who humble themselves will be exalted."

Luke 18:9–14 above is the perfect place to reflect upon here. This verse hints at the dangers of prosperity-based thinking.

Certainly, it isn't the case that each and every wealthy man is a self-righteous, self-obsessed fanatic. But if one begins to revolve the entirety of one's faith around the axis of material power and wealth, then one is surely heading down such a path.

The fault with much of the prosperity gospel is that instead of engaging with growth and prosperity of the *spirit*, much of this school focuses on progress and achievement of the *soul*. (As before, I use this distinction in a pragmatic, non-theologically loaded sense.) Realizing the obvious fact that this achievement was either indirectly or directly bestowed by God Himself, prosperity adherents rationalize that this achievement of the soul is "because of God's care for our success." Although this message surely misses the mark, its allure is understandable. Is it not easier to draw people into your ministry by preaching material success of the soul, as opposed to hard-fought success of the *spirit*?

We've seen the generic pitfalls of prosperity teaching, but what effect does this school of theology have upon society? For a glimpse into the sort of society that fuels such a theology of self-image and self-obsession, one need look no further than the so-called *Gilded Age* of the late nineteenth and early twentieth century. Kate Bowler gives us an excellent assessment in her *Blessed*:

> Mental magic surged in the late nineteenth century [. . .] The era after the Civil War, often known as the Gilded Age, witnessed a flood of religious ideals that bathed the period with hearty individualism and a bold pragmatism. *Self-mastery became an art and occupation, as people sought to consolidate the era's advances with improvements to their own lives. An ethos of self-help prevailed*: personal sewing machines and Popular Mechanics magazine bowed technology to house repair; a t the same time, gymnasiums appeared in universities and city centers across the country, as people devoted themselves to the pleasure and pursuit of self-taught athletic conditioning. (emphasis added)[9]

Bowler grants us some crucial perspective. We can see the emergence of the prosperity gospel as an extension of the greater theme of social and scientific "advance." With all of these advancements and new, fancy methods of exerting one's *will* upon the world, it is little surprise that such a worldview wriggled its way into the psyche of the Gilded Age man. This newfound obsession with the will manifested itself as unbridled ambition and extreme lack of concern for any societal consequences accompanying this pursuit.

Having landed on the topic of aggressive ambition and insidious inhibition, we might as well take another look at *politics*. What is the relation between modern political worldview and the Gilded Age's lust for material possession? What do us modern folks think about all of this?

For those Christians on the left side of the political aisle, it might be tempting to argue that there is some innate connection between malorientation of the soul and capitalism. It might be tempting to assume that

---

9. Bowler, *Blessed* (PhD thesis version), 28–29.

capitalism *itself* is to be blamed for Gilded Age-style opulence. However, there is absolutely no connection here. Let's see why.

Long story short: those who try to blame capitalism and conservativism for Gilded Age-style opulence confound *personal* and *societal* motivations. In other words, it is often falsely assumed that those people or politicians who proclaim themselves liberals or "left-wing" *personally* desire for social integration and genuine progress. In actuality—on *both* sides of the aisle—there is no necessary connection between one's professed ideals for society and one's motivations therebehind. To get a better grasp on this, let's take an example of a hypothetical head of state, call him "Ted."

Ted goes on various social media platforms and proclaims his penchant for globalism and "social justice" for all peoples, races and creeds. Ted is a "social justice" crusader! It seems as though these are his genuine desires and passions, to institute global unity and peace. However, behind closed doors—with his closest constituents—Ted readily admits that he doesn't care so much for globalism or social justice. These topics are simply the "hot-ticket" items he's calculated will catapult him to political stardom. Ted is an awesome and genuine guy, isn't he? Not.

Alas, there are numerous "Teds" across the globe, and their personal desires do not jive with their publically proclaimed views. Today, although we have moved beyond the unbridled and insatiable industrialism and quasi anarcho-capitalism of the Gilded Age, we certainly have not moved beyond the phenomenon of *political duplicitousness*. The sad fact is this: regardless of what ideology our politicians profess, their prime goal is the advancement of their own interests. When one forgets this, ideology is often unfairly demonized. Gilded Age or not, modern society's "self-interested" and ambitious are alive and well.

In this sense, one cannot sanely claim, "Yeah, the Gilded Age and its prosperity gospel values weren't great, but society has move beyond that now! It doesn't seem like today's 'prosperity gospel' is doing too bad after all." The prosperity gospel hasn't loosened its grip upon society since the Gilded Age. In many respects, it has only doubled down.

In the modern age, we find reinforcement of so-called prosperity-based values essentially everywhere we look. From buckets full of airbrushed selfies, bikini pics and new car posts on Instagram to the "humblebragging" and "flexing" found on Twitter feeds, our society runs on "success." One would be hard-pressed to find a single politician under the age of 65 without a Twitter or Instagram account. Modernity can latch onto and fuel a prosperity gospel-like interpretation of scripture for perpetuity. The age of peak vanity has nearly arrived.

Ok... but that's enough doom and gloom. Let's try to round all of this out now.

I discussed how a fully spiritually integrated society could look, in which each and every citizen possesses a unity of consciousness under Christ. I talked about the supreme importance of man-to-man covenant under the Lord. And we also saw how the interpretation of scripture associated with "prosperity gospel" theology can afflict society at large.

The question that now hangs over our heads and weighs heavily on our hearts is this: how are we to go about fixing things and bring society closer to God, in unification with His principles? Unfortunately, I won't be able to fully elaborate on the potential answers to this question quite yet. But I will do my best to introduce more than a few solid starting points.

PART II

Getting God Back into the World: A Preview

CHAPTER 6

What to Avoid

A GREAT EXAMPLE OF exactly what we *don't* want to be preaching can be found in the late minister and evangelist Reverend Ike's sermons. Ike was no doubt a powerful and charismatic figure; this is why so many people devoutly followed his teachings! Nonetheless, he exhibited a warped emphasis on utilizing (nearly *manipulating*) the Holy Spirit and Jesus for mere earthly and selfish pursuits. One of Reverend Ike's famous sayings was, "Don't wait for your pie in the sky by and by; have it now with ice cream and a cherry on top."[1] Far from this being a message of community-centered strength or success under Christ, this message rings of a call to bolster the *individual* man, focusing on building up his soul in the *now*.

I cannot unfairly heap blame upon Reverend Ike, as he was part of a far larger theological tradition, stretching back to the late nineteenth century. The title of the first man to fully incorporate the individual will and the "pocket-based" notion of Jesus as precious talismanic goes to a fellow named E.W. Kenyon, pastor of the New Covenant Baptist Church. Although I do not doubt Mr. Kenyon's genuine intentions to spread the Word, many of his ideas had a detrimental impact on the theological connection between God, Christ and man.

Before I talk more about Kenyon, we should quickly investigate some of his theological roots. Where exactly did the emphasis on the human will originate? One paradigm highly conducive to prosperity theology was called "New Thought." New Thought arose in the mid-nineteenth century

---

1. Bowler, *Blessed* (PhD thesis version), 93.

PART II: GETTING GOD BACK INTO THE WORLD: A PREVIEW

in the writings of Phineas Parkhurst Quimby of Lebanon, New Hampshire. Quimby channeled the philosophy passed down by the German doctor, Franz Mesmer, after whom "mesmerism" got its name.[2]

Mesmer was no Christian. It would even be a bit of a stretch to call him a theist. Mesmer seemed steadfastly *deist*—one who sees the physical "universe" and all of its laws as a creation of a supreme and indifferent watchmaker-like being. He even flirted with Taoist and Buddhist principles of thought. Mesmer adhered to the notion that there is some sort of "natural energy" pervading throughout and interpenetrating all living things, an idea he called "animal magnetism." Being a committed medical doctor, he implemented these metaphysical ideas on his patients, attempting to "tap into" the forces to induce healing.[3]

Non-Christ-rooted principles have countenanced Christian theology numerous times—from St. Augustine's use of Platonic philosophy to the influences of Aristotle's theory of the soul upon Aquinas's theology. But nowhere do we see as hard-hitting and dangerous of an impact as we do in New Thought's imprint upon modern theology. The Grecian philosophical influences of the ancient days were basically benign and debatably even beneficial. Unfortunately, the more recent influences have no doubt proved less than benign.

I'll now turn back to the topic of E.W. Kenyon's theology, deferring once more to Dr. Bowler's historical insight from her *Blessed*:

> Just as the atonement transferred legal authority from Satan to the faithful, the name of Jesus held forensic significance. Kenyon taught that Jesus transferred the "Power of Attorney" to all those who use his name. Prayer took on binding legal qualities as believers followed Jesus' formula: "If ye shall ask anything in my name, I will do it" (John 14:14). Kenyon replaced the word "ask" with "demand," since petitioners were entitled to the legal benefits of Jesus' name. The Holy Spirit became merely an assistant as Kenyon gave the credit for casting out demons, speaking in tongues, and curing disease to the rightful use of the name of Jesus.[4]

There is absolutely nothing wrong with the sentiment found in the popular Philippians 4:13—the reminder that God and Jesus can strengthen us beyond measure. However, when the power of the individual through

---

2. Bowler, *Blessed* (Oxford Press version), 13.
3. Bowler, *Blessed* (Oxford), 13–14.
4. Bowler, *Blessed* (Oxford Press version), 20.

Christ begins to supersede the imperative of fellowship and man-to-man covenant under Christ, then trouble is afoot.

In terms of material-oriented, individualistic theology, we find a perfect example in the teachings of Russell H. Conwell (1843 to 1925). Conwell was a Baptist minister and lawyer famous for his sermon, "Acre of Diamonds" in which he slickly welded together ambitious avarice and Christ's spiritual blessings. Conwell would stand atop the stage and gaze intently out into the sea of believers, telling them, "I say you ought to be rich; you have no right to be poor."[5] Conwell, in preaching to the ego and avarice of the individual, debased the power and sanctity of the community and city *as a whole*. He was preying upon the increasingly fissured consciousness of the modern believer. And, in retrospect, his theology has only served to magnify these mental divisions.

---

5. Bowler, *Blessed* (Oxford), 32.

CHAPTER 7

WHAT TO AIM FOR

Now the Lord is the Spirit; and where the Spirit of the Lord *is*, there *is* liberty. But we all, with unveiled face, beholding as in a mirror the glory of the Lord, are being transformed into the same image from glory to glory, just as by the Spirit of the Lord.

2 CORINTHIANS 3:17–18[1]

> **The Purpose of the Parables**
>
> **10** Then the disciples came and said to him, "Why do you speak to them in parables?" **11** And he answered them, "To you it has been given to know the secrets of the kingdom of heaven, but to them it has not been given. **12** For to the one who has, more will be given, and he will have an abundance, but from the one who has not, even what he has will be taken away. **13** This is why I speak to them in parables, because seeing they do not see, and hearing they do not hear, nor do they understand. **14** Indeed, in their case the prophecy of Isaiah is fulfilled that says:

MATTHEW 13:10–14 REMINDS US how much substance, how much "spiritual food" mere intellectual, inert knowledge lacks.

1. NKJV.

What to Aim For

A believer "knows" that God is the Almighty and that Jesus is man's Savior, but he/she may not truly believe what God and Jesus have to say to them. In other words, one can "believe in" God without truly *believing* Him. There is a profound difference between (i) believing in God and Jesus and (ii) believing in God and Jesus's *plan for your life*. Of course, we can't get to His plan for us without first penetrating sufficiently deep into scripture and theology. Without such penetration, there is a real danger that we will not be able to fully comprehend the extent of His plan for us.

We've seen above how much impact an errant or deviant interpretation of scripture can have upon the Christian community. From Kate Bowler's, *Blessed: A History of the American Prosperity Gospel*, we saw how a vein of spiritual restlessness can impact an entire community of faith. But we have only skimmed the surface in terms of such theological investigation. In order to eradicate the self-centered, fractured conscious-catering theology of our modern day, we will have to address various trends of the modern era. Then we must glimpse a compelling, anciently rooted, and communally motivated theological alternative.

This is no easy endeavor, but I will try to outline some of the essential steps. First and foremost, we must strike a proper balance between (i) *individualism* and *collectivism* and (ii) *soul*, *spirit* and *Spirit*.

After straightening out the above issues, we must then find a middle ground between two extremes. On one end there is the prosperity gospel-like *emphasis* on the physical and on the other a Gnostic-like *disdain* for the physical realm. We must find a way to restore the ancient emphasis on the community and the covenant. We must humble the modern man, without diminishing his connection to the Almighty.

In our brief overview of the New Thought movement and our discussion of its impact on the early nineteenth-century American Protestant theology, we can see the precarious shifting of balance between individualism and collectivism. We can see the teetering between the soul, the spirit and the Spirit. In this period, the *social individualism* that accompanied the rise of technology and the burgeoning material comforts had blossomed into *theological individualism*. These two "breeds" of individualism subsequently enforced one another in mutual feedback. In terms of the distinction I made between ADHD of the soul and ADHD of the spirit—in the transition from mere social individualism to theological individualism—we see a perfect example of a movement from the former to the latter. The "attention deficit" of the Gilded Age man's soul sprouted into the attention deficit of the modern man's spirit.

In individualism, we have something so deeply ingrained within modern culture and theology so as to be nearly *indistinguishable* from the undifferentiated background of one's conscious.

Individualism has been in the societal and intellectual current for so long that it has, in many cases, been simply taken as a given. But, once we take a closer look at this phenomenon, we will be able to finally apprehend all of its influence on modern theology. We will be one step closer to fashioning a modern theology of spiritual unification under Christ, as opposed to one of cutthroat egotism and individualism.

I can't yet commence a full-on analytical dive into social and theological individualism. For now, I'll be content to simply outline our *vision* of a new, unified modern theology.

My "mission statement" is that we must develop a theology that fulfills the following requirements (among various others):

- Properly balances (i) the spiritual power of the *induvial* through Christ and the Spirt, (ii) the power of Christ and the Spirit *for God's Plan* and (iii) the spiritual power of *society*, comprising man-to-man covenants, through Christ and the Spirit. A level of abstraction higher than this, properly recognizes the power of (iii) to positively accentuate *both* (i) and (ii)

- Does not place undue emphasis upon the power of man's *soul* (his mental, volitional and emotional capacities), as opposed to his *spirit* (his Spirit-connected capacities)

- Does not debase Christ to a sort of genie to be rubbed for the purposes of one's own personal, material satisfaction

- Addresses the modern fissuring of man's consciousness and its spiritual ramifications and makes genuine attempts to take humanity back to a more unified and balanced spiritual state

- Not only does the above but also completes the above through the societal channeling of Christ and the Spirit, with due emphasis on man-to-man covenant, social responsibility, and collective temperance

With a theology that adheres to these principles, modern society will be better able to commune with the Lord. We will be better equipped to fulfill His Plan.

PART III

FOUNDATIONS OF A LIVING WORD

CHAPTER 8

No Spiritual Cushions

"We are the Bibles the world is reading; we are the creeds the world is needing; we are the sermons the world is heeding."

—Billy Graham[1]

Between roughly 1500 BC and 95 AD the Bible was an emerging work. The Book was meticulously and near continuously communicated from God to man, penetrating into each and every period of time and culture involved. By simply considering the perspective of those ancient folk—living and breathing in a world *without* a fully completed Book—we can glean some fascinating things about the ancient interaction between faith and everyday life.

In the modern day, it is often difficult to see Biblical stories as anything more than that—mere *stories*. Taking interpretative inspiration from modern media and literary trope, we often abstract away the personal, cultural and historical aspects at work within the Book. This leaves us with little more than curious, tall-seeming tales, involving people whom we could never hope to meet in the flesh. What we often forget is that these people were *real* to the Lord, and they inhabited very real cultural and historical places.

---

1. The source of this Graham quote unfortunately seems just as ethereal as modern society's conformance to it.

Part III: Foundations of a Living Word

If we wish to be confronted with the bare reality of ancient life, there is no better place to begin than Proverbs. The book of Proverbs is lined with verses directed towards diligence and what's known today as "work ethic." But, after considering these verses in context, it becomes clear that the ancient emphasis on work and diligence was of a fundamentally different kind than the modern one.

Below we see a sampling of the many verses related to idleness in Proverbs:

- 6:6-11 | Go to the ant, O sluggard; consider her ways, and be wise. Without having any chief, officer, or ruler, she prepares her bread in summer and gathers her food in harvest. How long will you lie there, O sluggard? When will you arise from your sleep? A little sleep, a little slumber, a little folding of the hands to rest, ...
- 10:5 | He who gathers in summer is a prudent son, but he who sleeps in harvest is a son who brings shame.
- 10:26 | Like vinegar to the teeth and smoke to the eyes, so is the sluggard to those who send him.
- 12:24 | The hand of the diligent will rule, while the slothful will be put to forced labor.
- 13:4 | The soul of the sluggard craves and gets nothing, while the soul of the diligent is richly supplied.
- 18:9 | Whoever is slack in his work is a brother to him who destroys.
- 20:4 | The sluggard does not plow in the autumn; he will seek at harvest and have nothing.
- 21:25 | The desire of the sluggard kills him, for his hands refuse to labor.

In these verses we see a stern yet Spirit-infused exhortation to remain diligent and motivated, lest an insidious idleness creep into the mind of man.

Although many moderns may try to compare these verses to the "self-help" mantras that have become ever popular, the emphasis of these verses is decidedly different than that of the latter. In order to best see this difference of emphasis, all we must do is browse through some of the modern age's best "self-help" tidbits. These quotes paradigmatically embody the modern "power of the will!"

No Spiritual Cushions

For example, we have the following:

- "Let others lead small lives, but not you. Let others argue over small things, but not you. Let others cry over small hurts, but not you. Let others leave their future in someone else's hands, but not you." —Jim Rohn
- "Destiny is as destiny does. If you believe you have no control, then you have no control." —Wess Roberts
- "You willed yourself to where you are today, so will yourself out of it." —Stephen Richards
- "Your inner strength is your outer foundation" —Alan Rufus

To the modern mind—even to the modern *believer's* mind—it might not be immediately apparent what the difference is between these quotes and the Proverbs verses above.

Let's see if I can distill things. To put it succinctly—the above quotations focus on the building up of man *through the man,* while the Proverbs verses focus on the nourishing of man's spirit and soul *through reverence for the Lord* and His Plan. One set of words soothes the ego. The other tames it.

Moving back to the discussion of the modern man's "fractured consciousness," we can see how the "self-hope" quotations ultimately bow and collapse under the weight of the modern conscious and all of its superfluous bells and whistles. Any time man seeks personal progress through himself, erecting a structure of success and achievement around solely *his* will-power, his journey is nullified from the outset. There is a world of difference between mere human meaning and Holy Meaning.

Without a solid undergirding of spiritual purpose, without the recognition that there is a higher Plan and the subsequent humbling of the individual's own plan, man is doomed to self-obsession and subsequent self-righteousness. Romans 10:3 serves as a perfect example here—"For, being ignorant of the righteousness of God, and seeking to establish their own, they did not submit to God's righteousness."[2]

One need not be an atheist or agnostic to possess such ignorance of the righteousness of God, perhaps contrary to modern opinion. In terms of our discussion of the "prosperity gospel" in previous chapters, I should say that preachers and followers of such a theology often dangle precariously over the edge of a spiritual cliff. One of their legs is safely nourished by the

2. ESV.

PART III: FOUNDATIONS OF A LIVING WORD

Spirit while the other hangs in self-conceit over a chasm of self-righteousness. When our theology prescribes us all to be "little gods" of our own, the Plan is debased and held hostage to the plans of man.

In self-righteousness, there paradoxically lies a whirling spout of *self-hatred*. If the self-righteous one happens to be poor or be lacking in one way or another then he will likely hate himself. And in hating himself he will end up *hating his Lord*.

If one bases the entirety of his life around his own will, whenever he is down and out of "luck," he will self-centeredly blame his own will for all of his woes. He will neglect to submit or repent. And he will fail to avert his eyes from the world, up towards to Spirit. The problem with this sort of man is that he continues on believing that he *alone*—through his meager, human will—has to power to shape his life and its impact upon the world.

It is here that we reach the paradigmatic example of trial and temptation of the human will: the book of Job. Let's start out with the word of man, the words of the *will*:

Job 8   New International Version

Bildad

8 Then Bildad the Shuhite replied:

2   "How long will you say such things?
        Your words are a blustering wind.
3   Does God pervert justice?
        Does the Almighty pervert what is right?
4   When your children sinned against him,
        he gave them over to the penalty of their sin.
5   But if you will seek God earnestly
        and plead with the Almighty,
6   if you are pure and upright,
        even now he will rouse himself on your behalf
        and restore you to your prosperous state.

In the voice of Bildad we hear a materialistic, will-based spirit of temptation calling out to Job. In the context of Job's spiritually journey, Bildad represents the iniquitous urge of outburst and resentment. Bildad's role was to sufficiently irk Job, getting him to divert his attention away from the Spirit, towards the *material world* and its earthly passions. In this sense, Bildad taps into the essence of the serpent through which man is told, "Well, if God were so good, would he really forbid you or punish you?" behind a wry and crafty smile.

If Job had been a self-obsessed, self-righteous man, he would have responded to the proddings of Bildad in quite the predictable manner. A self-righteous Job would have received a faux revelation and called out to God in indignation, *demanding* that his case be reviewed.

"God, I *know* you have made some mistake!! I *demand* that you look at my heart again!"

Fortunately for Job, his heart was sufficiently Spirit-filled to deter him from such a blasphemous outburst. For all his begging and beseeching, Job never attacked God or His Plan. In fact—though it may seem to many that Job aggressively questioned God's Plan—Job's dialogue with the Lord can be seen as a sort of dialectical progression, a journey culminating in mental and spiritual enlightenment.

Job

9 Then Job replied:

2 "Indeed, I know that this is true.
   But how can mere mortals prove their innocence before God?
3 Though they wished to dispute with him,
   they could not answer him one time out of a thousand.
4 His wisdom is profound, his power is vast.
   Who has resisted him and come out unscathed?
5 He moves mountains without their knowing it
   and overturns them in his anger.
6 He shakes the earth from its place
   and makes its pillars tremble.

In each of Job's pleadings, he retains the Lord as his Almighty. Job never neglects to acknowledge His omniscience, omnipotence, and omnibenevolence.

Here's something very important to keep in mind: if Satan were to get his way, Job would not merely question the Lord; he would *confront* His very Being.

In terms of our previous comparison between the verses of Proverbs and the "self-help" quotes of modernity, we can see how both sets of quotes intertwine with the core lessons of the book of Job, both in vastly differing ways.

Let's say that the great American entrepreneur from the above quotes, Jim Rohn, were born into the body of an ancient man in the days of Job. Let's imagine for a second that this ancient "entrepreneur" had an intimate connection with Job and consoled and counseled him regularly. One night, as Job was expressing his spiritual struggles to the ancient Rohn, he said to him, "You know Job, let *others* lead small lives, but not *you*. Let *others* argue over small things, but not *you*. Let *others* cry over small hurts, but not *you*. Let others leave their future in someone else's hands, but not *you*." Rohn then left him to consider the implications. How would this have impacted Job?

This mini motivational talk—for all of its inspiration and passion—had no mention of the Lord or Christ, nonetheless any sort of *humbling* of man before God. If this sort of message were given to Job before he was afflicted, it could have easily wormed its way into his heart and spawned a cadre of thick and prideful vines over his soul and spirit.

This is not the only way in which such a self-help monologue could have tripped up Job's spirit. Let's imagine now that the leadership author from the above self-help quotes, Wes Roberts, took the place of Bildad and stealthily bestowed upon Job his worldly knowledge. Perhaps he would say, "Job, how long is this going to continue? This is ridiculous man! Destiny is as destiny does. If you believe you have no control, then you have no control!" Job turns his face down and squints with concentration for a moment and then one of Wes Roberts's friends comes over and offers the following: "You know, Job, I think Wes is exactly right . . . You willed yourself to where you are today, so will yourself out of it." Job sits there for a moment more, squinting still and feeling increasingly lost in his skull. Several seconds later he clasps his fists together and begins to shake with rage.

Rage . . . *against the Lord*.

Another paradigmatic example of the clash between the ego and the Will is found in 1 Corinthians.

No Spiritual Cushions

1 Corinthians 14   New International Version

Intelligibility in Worship

14 Follow the way of love and eagerly desire gifts of the Spirit, especially prophecy. **2** For anyone who speaks in a tongue[a] does not speak to people but to God. Indeed, no one understands them; they utter mysteries by the Spirit. **3** But the one who prophesies speaks to people for their strengthening, encouraging and comfort. **4** Anyone who speaks in a tongue edifies themselves, but the one who prophesies edifies the church. **5** I would like every one of you to speak in tongues,[b] but I would rather have you prophesy. The one who prophesies is greater than the one who speaks in tongues,[c] unless someone interprets, so that the church may be edified.

The Bible does no doubt uphold the spiritual value to be found in the speaking of tongues. However—contra the modern doctrine (read: *dogma*) of the various veins of the prosperity gospel—this spiritual gift ultimately pales in comparison to the establishment of genuine *fellowship* and brotherly *covenant* under the Lord. As to the question of the endurance of the gift of tongues into the modern age, I will decline to pass judgement.

Just before these verses, Paul eloquently illustrates the ideal of Spiritual Love that Christ craves for our lives. Paul says, "Love never stops loving. It extends beyond the gift of prophecy, which eventually fades away. It is more enduring than tongues, which will one day fall silent. Love remains long after words of knowledge are forgotten. Our present knowledge and our prophecies are but partial, but when love's perfection arrives, the partial will fade away."[3]

Let's see if we fully comprehend that . . . *Love* is more enduring than mere spiritual knowledge. *Love* is the perfection that even the *grandest of prophecies* could never hope to attain! In our modern day, so many of us believers are so deeply focused on matters of the soul, matters that we think will bring *us* success. Genuine, selfless love is far too often a secondary consideration.

Just in these two instances alone, in Job's story and Paul's exhortations, we can see how profoundly the average modern-day believer *fails* the test of the living Word.

---

3. 1 Corinthians 13:8–10 TPT.

PART III: Foundations of a Living Word

Put differently, were the modern man placed in the shoes of an ancient man and subsequently led to a real, breathing instance of scripture in the making, he would have trouble filling the role as "actor" in the Word. I might go so far as to say this—had there never been a single ancient man able to fill the role of "actor in the Word," it is doubtful that the average modern man could step in, fill his shoes, and channel the living scripture.

This is terrifying to think about.

CHAPTER 9

NO SPIRITUAL LUXURY WITHOUT *SPIRITUAL* SUBMISSION

"I appeal to you therefore, brothers, by the mercies of God, to present your bodies as a living sacrifice, holy and acceptable to God, which is your spiritual worship. Do not be conformed to this world, but be transformed by the renewal of your mind, that by testing you may discern what is the will of God, what is good and acceptable and perfect."
—ROMANS 12:1–2[1]

"Behold, to obey is better than sacrifice . . ."
—1 SAMUEL 15:22[2]

OUR MODERN WORLD HAS a complicated relationship with the word "sacrifice."

Many a well-dressed, meticulously groomed businessman and many a highly trained doctor and shrewd lawyer think that they have availed themselves of this word and concept long ago. To the modern man, the standard

1. ESV.
2. ESV.

reply to the question of what exactly sacrifice is goes something like this—"Sacrifice is simply an investment for your own success. If you choose your investments wisely, put in the work, and stay vigilant, then you'll achieve everything you've always wanted!" This sentiment resonates viscerally with the modern "self-sufficient" and "self-made" man.

Looking back at the collection of self-help quotes I presented, such pieces of superficial nourishment as "Destiny is as destiny does. If you believe you have no control, then you have no control" and "Your inner strength is your outer foundation" give credence to the notion that sacrifice is fundamentally *self-centered*.

Interestingly enough, there are ancient roots of this self-centered philosophy of success running deeply through modern society—those of *Stoicism*. The philosophy of ancient Stoicism has influenced modern man so much that there is even a hugely popular eponymous website, "Daily Stoic," claiming to provide the modern man with "Ancient wisdom for everyday life." There are scores of books centered on the wisdom of the stoics, perhaps the most prominent being, *How to Think Like a Roman Emperor: The Stoic Philosophy of Marcus Aurelius* (2019).[3]

To get a grip on what it is that "Daily Stoic," and the overall landscape of modern Stoicism bring to the table, we need look no further than the assorted quotes of the Roman emperor, Marcus Aurelius, one of Stoicism's earliest adherents.

- Waste no more time arguing what a good man should be. Be One.
- Think of the life you have lived until now as over and, as a dead man, see what's left as a bonus and live it according to Nature. Love the hand that fate deals you and play it as your own, for what could be more fitting?
- If it is not right, do not do it, if it is not true, do not say it.
- Choose not to be harmed — and you won't feel harmed. Don't feel harmed — and you haven't been.
- External things are not the problem. It's your assessment of them. Which you can erase right now.[4]

To the strong-willed and healthy egoed modern, these quotes may seem insightful and penetrating. Alas, the only merit of these words is that

[3]. Robertson, St. Martin's Publishing.
[4]. See Needleman and Piazza's, *The Essential Marcus Aurelius*.

which is left behind after the purity of the Spirit has been skimmed off. Emperor Aurelius was wise. But he lacked Christ.

On this note we should revisit a statement made several chapters ago regarding the will and self-righteousness:

> Simply speaking, there is *no* restriction that idolatry be something *external* to one's self. Idolatry, especially in modern times, can *invade one's heart* and embed itself deeply within the soul, siphoning off the Spirit and transducing its message into warped and egotistical fantasy. In the case of prosperity theology, the idol isn't necessarily the physical money. The idol is the personal will, the self-image and the self-esteem. When these elements are mixed without temperance, *self-righteousness* is often the resulting cocktail.

Just as is the case in prosperity theology, the idol of Stoicism is not even anything physical. The idol of the stoic man is his own will-power. Temperance means nothing if the will and ego and left to run roughshod over whatever superficial signs of humility the stoic countenance bears. This is nothing more than a fact of history—a society cannot place full emphasis upon the will of the individual man and neglect to emphasize the Lord and His covenants. Such a society runs the heavy risk of imploding into an internecine wasteland. This is part of what we're seeing in action in the modern day.

The modern stoic and the self-help guru would have you believe that sacrifice is first and foremost a tool of self-empowerment. In both the stoic and the self-help philosophy, the capacity of the *will* is emphasized to an utterly absurd degree. Adherents hold steadfast to the words of a self-interested Roman emperor, "Choose not to be harmed — and you won't feel harmed. Don't feel harmed — and you haven't been."[5] It is through such self-obsession that stoics and self-help fanatics can fully insulate themselves from their spiritual brothers and sisters at large. Both of these folks run the risk of turning inwards and playing a masturbatory game of "tame the will," neglecting to care about their *communities*. After all, if it's all about man's will, what is the point in communal enrichment or societal reflection?

Here we are brought back to Apostle Paul's key words about the relationship between personal strengthening and communal outreach.

---

5. Needleman and Piazza's, *The Essential Marcus Aurelius*.

PART III: Foundations of a Living Word

1 Corinthians 14 New International Version

Intelligibility in Worship

14 Follow the way of love and eagerly desire gifts of the Spirit, especially prophecy. **2** For anyone who speaks in a tongue[a] does not speak to people but to God. Indeed, no one understands them; they utter mysteries by the Spirit. **3** But the one who prophesies speaks to people for their strengthening, encouraging and comfort. **4** Anyone who speaks in a tongue edifies themselves, but the one who prophesies edifies the church. **5** I would like every one of you to speak in tongues,[b] but I would rather have you prophesy. The one who prophesies is greater than the one who speaks in tongues,[c] unless someone interprets, so that the church may be edified.

It is not merely the case that the modern stoics have missed a spiritual point here or there. These folks neglect the most crucial spiritual point of all—the supreme importance of spiritual *surrender*. It is here that I turn to our Savior:

> Then Jesus said to his disciples, "Whoever wants to be my disciple must deny themselves and take up their cross and follow me. For whoever wants to save their life will lose it, but whoever loses their life for me will find it. What good will it be for someone to gain the whole world, yet forfeit their soul? Or what can anyone give in exchange for their soul? For the Son of Man is going to come in his Father's glory with his angels, and then he will reward each person according to what they have done.
> —MATTHEW 16:24–27[6]

Despite all the wisdom the modern stoics and self-helpers think they have attained, Proverbs 1:7 reminds us that they have completely missed the point: "The fear of the Lord is the beginning of knowledge; fools despise wisdom and instruction."[7] Notice what this says about what "wisdom" and "instruction" really are. Wisdom—contra the stoics and the self-helpers—is that which rests upon the Will, not the flimsy and fickle human will. And instruction is that which one receives with one's personal pride set aside.

---

6. ESV.
7. ESV.

No Spiritual Luxury Without Spiritual Submission

It seems that this all comes down to man's innate longing for *perfection*. Deep down, we all long for spiritual and physical perfection, whether or not we have been blessed with the God-given *wisdom* to discern what perfect actually entails. It might sound strange to say that "we all long for spiritual and physical perfection." We *all*? We're tempted to question, "You mean to tell me that even non-believers desire 'spiritual perfection'?" This is where the distinction between *craving* and *desire* can help us out tremendously. To answer the question, we might say that even non-believers *crave* spiritual perfection. The fact is that they have not yet been blessed with the wisdom to *desire* it.

It will be helpful to make a list of verses comprising these two concepts, in order to see what more clearly what I mean. Notice that, generally speaking, desire can have both good and bad connotations. In our usage, "craving" will be associated with longings of the earthly flesh and "desire" will be Christ-rooted.

Craving	Desire
HEWBREWS 13:5 | Keep your life free from love of money, and be content with what you have, for he has said, "I will never leave you nor forsake you."	PSALM 37:4 | Delight yourself in the Lord, and he will give you the desires of your heart.
1 TIMOTHY 6:10 | For the love of money is a root of all kinds of evils. It is through this craving that some have wandered away from the faith and pierced themselves with many pangs.	PROVERBS 10:24 | What the wicked dreads will come upon him, but the desire of the righteous will be granted.
PROVERBS 20:1 | Wine is a mocker, strong drink a brawler, and whoever is led astray by it is not wise.	PSALM 119:20 | My soul is consumed with longing for your rules at all times.
EXODUS 20:17 | "You shall not covet your neighbor's house; you shall not covet your neighbor's wife, or his male servant, or his female servant, or his ox, or his donkey, or anything that is your neighbor's."	1 JOHN 2:15-17 | Do not love the world or the things in the world. If anyone loves the world, the love of the Father is not in him. For all that is in the world—the desires of the flesh and the desires of the eyes and pride in possessions—is not from the Father but is from the world. And the world is passing away along with its desires, but whoever does the will of God abides forever.

PART III: Foundations of a Living Word

1 PETER 1:24-25 | For "All flesh is like grass and all its glory like the flower of grass. The grass withers, and the flower falls, but the word of the Lord remains forever." And this word is the good news that was preached to you.	JEREMIAH 29:13 | You will seek me and find me, when you seek me with all your heart.[8]

Juxtaposing these concepts, we can clearly see how different they are. Considering these in conjunction with the fractured consciousness of the modern man, we see how hard it can be for him to not only grok this distinction but to put it into *action*. We live in an unfortunate age in which the "pagans" chase unbridledly after cloying pleasure and the devout often seek to flagellate every earthly urge from their flesh. It is imperative we find a spiritual *middle ground* in all of this. As we can see above, desire is actually a spiritually beneficial (read: necessary) thing.

Despite the modern age's heady hedonism and fervent worship of achievement and success, if we pan in close enough, we can just make out the cries of lost and aching souls. In Michael Horton's first volume of his brilliant work of theology and history, *Justification* (2018), he shows us just how this works:

> Robert Jay Lifton, a psychiatrist and pioneer in brain research, observes that the source of many neuroses in society today is a nagging sense of guilt without knowing its source. The anxiety is "a vague but persistent kind of self-condemnation related to the symbolic disharmonies I've described, a sense of having no outlet for his loyalties and no symbolic structure for his achievements." I interpret this theologically as suggesting that there is no external law to measure oneself by or external gospel through which one becomes re-scripted "in-Christ." "Rather than being a feeling of evil or sinfulness," he says, "it takes the form of a nagging sense of unworthiness all the more troublesome for its lack of clear origin."[9]

This reaches down to a fundamental fact known since nearly the dawn of civilization: no matter how many riches and pleasures one accumulates, if he never finds true *meaning* for himself, he will never be fully satisfied deep within. It can be quite difficult indeed for even the believer to find *bona fide* meaning in such an age as today.

---

8. All verses ESV.
9. Horton, *Justification*, 22.

No Spiritual Luxury Without Spiritual Submission

I will turn once more to Michael Horton's *Justification* for some beautiful explanation of this point:

> The Reformation debate seems to pale in the face of the outright Pelagian anthropological assumptions of the modern age, aptly summarized as "moralistic, therapeutic deism." Within a therapeutic outlook, even when the old terms are used, they acquire new meanings. Sin becomes dysfunction, and redemption is code for recovery. Peace with God—and with each other through that primary relationship—is not denied; it is just absent.[10]

This is a brilliant summary of much of modern theology and dogma—"moralistic, therapeutic deism."

The *moralism* comes from the rigid reliance on the power of one's will and ego. The *therapy* comes from the emphasis on self-help and self-empowerment for personal success. The *deism* comes from the lack of proper integration of God, The Spirit and the Son into everyday life.

Now back to the craving|desiring dichotomy I offered. When we meditate upon the meanings of these words—in conjunction with the meanings of *moralism, therapy* and *deism*—we reach some very interesting and insightful theological conclusions.

This is the essential tension raging within the modern psyche: the battle between the *impulses* and the *will*. For the average modern-day man, the mind is a two-faculty entity, comprising only two competing sub-entities. One of these sub-entities is that which leads one astray and away from one's personal goals. The other of these entities is that which has the power to tame this other, wild entity. These two entities are akin to Plato's twin forces of emotion and reason. But the modern knows them as *desire* and *will*.

The internet is replete with toy articles and programs touting the transformative powers of man's will, from "The Science of Willpower: How to Train Your Productivity Muscle." (Medium.com) to "How to Increase Willpower and Be Mentally Tough" (Lifehack.com). It seems that there is no ill that cannot be fixed by will!

To many "life coaches" and "self-help speakers," the most fundamental human dichotomy is that between the *will* and the *desires*. If one can somehow learn how to master the former, one will never again be subjected to the assassination of their aspirations by their fickle desires. This is the essence of the modern "self-made man."

---

10. Horton, *Justification*, 27–28.

PART III: Foundations of a Living Word

Desires and urges, on the other hand, are things to be quashed and desperately re-directed, as is evinced by such article names as "How to overcome a strong desire? Just D.E.A.L with it." and "Controlling Your Desires Is The Basis For Personal Power, And Its Mastery Is The Payoff."

It is this division of the modern mind into "will" and "desire" that helps to furnish the descriptor of "moralistic, therapeutic deism."

In terms of emphasis, it would perhaps be more accurate to describe the spiritual ambience of the average modern believer as *therapeutic*, moralistic deism. First and foremost, the modern man is told to take care of himself. One of the most popular modern self-help platitudes is "Be selfish for once!" As if we humans need to be *reminded* to be selfish!

It is in this sense that the will of the modern is directed inwards, exhorted to "therapeutically" focus on his own "progress" and "success." It is also in this very same sense that moralism rears its ugly head, as those recently out of self-help "therapy" begin to view their social world as a *hierarchy* lined with those ostensibly stronger in will-power and those "weaker."

With all of the rigorous "training of the will" undergone by the average modern man, the set of moral codes and dictums that once resided out in the world and in cultures has been *internalized*, crammed into the skulls of those viciously eager to will their way to personal gain. The modern man is a cool, calculating machine brimming with self-interested strategy and mechanisms of ego protection. With this modern internalization of law, it becomes quite tricky indeed to discern our own relationships with moralism and rigid, law-like adherence. With this sort of set up, it becomes rather easy to say, "I'm not being spiritually rigid at all! Which laws am I clinging to and putting before God?"

The point is that one needn't adhere to any *external*, political or social laws at all in order to be rigid and legalistic of spirit. On this note let us return again to a point I've made several times now; it's just that crucial:

> Simply speaking, there is *no* restriction that idolatry be something *external* to one's self. Idolatry, especially in modern times, can *invade one's heart* and embed itself deeply within the soul, siphoning off the Spirit and transducing its message into warped and egotistical fantasy. In the case of the prosperity gospel, the idol isn't even the physical money. The idol is the personal will, the self-image and the self-esteem. And, when these elements are mixed without temperance, *self-righteousness* is the resulting cocktail.

No Spiritual Luxury Without Spiritual Submission

Fortunately, we need not dig very deep to find numerous scriptural antidotes to these modern ills. Bellow, I list some of the most relevant, those that remind the believer to abandon all rigidity, external *and* internal.

- MATTHEW 10:39: Whoever finds his life will lose it, and whoever loses his life for my sake will find it.

- 1 TIMOTHY 6:5–8: And constant friction among people who are depraved in mind and deprived of the truth, imagining that godliness is a means of gain. Now there is great gain in godliness with contentment, for we brought nothing into the world, and we cannot take anything out of the world. But if we have food and clothing, with these we will be content.

- JOHN 15:1–7: "I am the true vine, and my Father is the vinedresser. Every branch in me that does not bear fruit he takes away, and every branch that does bear fruit he prunes, that it may bear more fruit. Already you are clean because of the word that I have spoken to you. Abide in me, and I in you. As the branch cannot bear fruit by itself, unless it abides in the vine, neither can you, unless you abide in me. I am the vine; you are the branches. Whoever abides in me and I in him, he it is that bears much fruit, for apart from me you can do nothing. . . .

- 1 PETER 5:7: Casting all your anxieties on him, because he cares for you.

- LUKE 22:42: Saying, "Father, if you are willing, remove this cup from me. Nevertheless, not my will, but yours, be done."[11]

---

11. All ESV.

CHAPTER 10

Life is The Gift

For if we live, we live to the Lord, and if we die, we die to the Lord. So then, whether we live or whether we die, we are the Lord's.

—ROMANS 14:8[1]

And the dust returns to the earth as it was, and the spirit returns to God who gave it.

— ECCLESIASTES 12:7[2]

Let's start with an eye-opener:

> In response to the Black Death of 1348–50, the Church of England called for weeks of special prayers and fasting. However, in the 1980s, the church called for more government funding for medical research.[3]

This is a highly insightful excerpt from Michael Horton's *Justification* (2018). This perspective is enough to make us seriously contemplate

1. ESV.
2. ESV.
3. Horton, *Justification*, 19.

the kind of theological world we live in. It brings many questions to the believer's mind. Why does the modern church focus less on bodily and spiritual submission? Why are we content to insulate ourselves from the bare and often harsh reality of God and Christ Jesus? And, above all—what has made us want to insulate ourselves from spiritual reality?

These are heady questions. I surely cannot answer them in the blink of an eye. What I can do, though, is try to distill them into a single topic. I can package them together under one extremely important idea—spiritual gifts and "cessationsim versus continuationism." This topic might appear somewhat tangential, but it cuts straight to the core issues of modern theology. The implications of this topic tell us that something has eroded the modern believer's heart so thoroughly and crushingly that there is no deep, spiritual difference between the two stances. After all, *both* the cessationist and the continuationist call for "government funding for medical research" over "weeks of special prayers and fasting." We are all more similar than we would like to believe.

"Cessationsim versus continuationism" is the debate in which we Christians argue about whether *spiritual gifts* are available to the *modern* man. The cessationist is convinced that so-called gifts of the spirit no longer apply, while the continuationist is convinced they do still apply. Alas, shining through both these positions are the most popular theological poisons of the modern age—self-importance and reckless individualism.

Michael Horton explains this modern undercurrent nicely:

> Drawing on this example, sociologist Steve Bruce explains, "Individualism, egalitarianism, liberal democracy, and science and technology all contribute to a general sense of self-importance, of freedom from fate." Consequently, "In the world of the mainstream churches and in the cultic milieu of alternative spirituality people are now generally unwilling to subordinate themselves to an external authority."[4]

On the face of things, we would hope that the continuationist would push past the "self-importance" and obstinacy of the modern age. We would hope that one who believes he (and every other believer) has the power to attune the world to the glory of Christ would abandon worldly influence. We would hope he would desire a raw, undiluted form of Christianity. We would *hope*. . .

---

4. Horton, *Justification*, 19.

PART III: Foundations of a Living Word

The fact is, it makes no difference where one falls. Continuationist and cessationist alike, theology has yielded to the idle comforts of modernity, for better and for worse. The safe haven that is modern society has insulated the believer from the bare realities of physical life. And, as a consequence, modern spirituality has itself been detached from its bucolic ancestral roots.

The acceptance of the importance of the gifts of the Spirit is *not enough* for the modern man to overcome his self-centered and individualistic tendencies. Nearly the entire modern "prosperity gospel" is case in point. More encouragingly though, the lack of acceptance of the gifts is by no means a damning blow to the modern believer. The most important thing to realize is that *neither* continuationism nor cessationsim is enough to jolt the modern believer out of his slumber of "therapeutic, moralistic deism."

The question, of course, is now "Well, what must we do to jolt the modern man out of this lackluster theological state?" For this, we will have to dig into the nature of the gifts themselves. In this regard, there is no better place to begin than 1 Corinthians 12.

> 7 The Holy Spirit is given to each of us in a special way. That is for the good of all. 8 To some people the Spirit gives a message of wisdom. To others the same Spirit gives a message of knowledge. 9 To others the same Spirit gives faith. To others that one Spirit gives gifts of healing. 10 To others he gives the power to do miracles. To others he gives the ability to prophesy. To others he gives the ability to tell the spirits apart. To others he gives the ability to speak in different kinds of languages they had not known before. And to still others he gives the ability to explain what was said in those languages. 11 All the gifts are produced by one and the same Spirit. He gives gifts to each person, just as he decides.

Of course, if one is blitzing through the Bible like it's a mass market mystery novel, this section will read with a connotation of egotism and will-centrism. In this manner, even the diehard continuationists can quite easily fall victim to overly individualistic and borderline moralistic thinking. Fortunately, there is always another chance for a closer read, and Paul places a gorgeous bit of wisdom right after this presentation of the myriad gifts of the Spirit:

LIFE IS THE GIFT

One Body but Many Parts

> **12** There is one body, but it has many parts. But all its many parts make up one body. It is the same with Christ. **13** We were all baptized by one Holy Spirit. And so we are formed into one body. It didn't matter whether we were Jews or Gentiles, slaves or free people. We were all given the same Spirit to drink. **14** So the body is not made up of just one part. It has many parts.
>
> **15** Suppose the foot says, "I am not a hand. So I don't belong to the body." By saying this, it cannot stop being part of the body. **16** And suppose the ear says, "I am not an eye. So I don't belong to the body." By saying this, it cannot stop being part of the body. **17** If the whole body were an eye, how could it hear? If the whole body were an ear, how could it smell? **18** God has placed each part in the body just as he wanted it to be. **19** If all the parts were the same, how could there be a body? **20** As it is, there are many parts. But there is only one body.

The obvious theme of Paul's prose is the unity of sons and daughters under Christ. Unfortunately, it seems that this may be the *only* salient point that many moderns take away from the section. It is one thing to recognize that we are all equal under Christ and encouraged to take part in His Salvation. It is another thing entirely to realize what is going on "below the surface" here, socially and communally.

Not only does Paul aim to remind the Corinthians of their unity under their Savior, but he also intends to draw them together, *socially* and *politically*. It is extremely important to mention the kind of social milieu Corinth had in these days; it will remind us more than a little of some of our own modern cities and towns. Stephen T. Um in his 1 *Corinthians: The Word of the Cross (Preaching the Word)* gives us an excellent introduction to things:

> Corinth was an *aspirational* city. Its citizens were looking to advance on the ladder of upward social mobility, and they did this by aspiring to affluence for the sake of establishing their own honor. "The core community and core tradition of the city culture were those of trade, business, entrepreneurial pragmatism in the pursuit

of success," and "perhaps no city in the Empire offered so congenial an atmosphere for individual and corporate advancement."[5]

This city is insanely familiar to us! On the one hand we have the rampant individualism and egotism, and on the other hand we have the superficial "diversity" and "acceptance." Such a city is a perfect picture of the modern "liberal" ideal—a secularized, individualized utopia of unbridled hedonism.

Just like Cain, we modern folks seek desperately to burry our longings, our *good desires* for Christ and *spiritual* safety. What better way is there to burry your visceral and spiritual desires than to drown them out with sensual pleasures and personal, egotistic successes? It is in this way that us moderns grow further and further away from the gravity of the Word and the sheer spiritual weight of Christ. It is in this manner that the Lord who once held dominion over the mind and heart of the pious ancient is reduced to a meticulously chiseled pocket figurine, crafted to be pulled out in times of fear and unease.

Martyrdom is as alienated from the modern way of life as the modern megachurch would have been from the ancients. Let that sink in . . . In an age when self-therapy reigns supreme, even the mere thought of self-sacrifice *without* material self-gain can seem gratuitously painful. This is a sacrifice that not even the noble stoics would dare to make.

The key point of this all flies far above our modern heads. The point is that man could never hope to achieve such a feat as martyrdom through the power of his meager human will alone! When one is operating through his own will, there is simply no incentive or volitionary force strong enough to keep him fully submitted to Christ and his Lord. The only possible way man can martyr is through the Will of the Lord.

On this note, we will visit some of the most profound words (outside of scripture itself) written about the intimate relationship between God and His children. Jacques Ellul, in his *The Meaning of the City*, traces the spiritual intricacies at play in the establishment of the city, that which stands as a beacon of man's will and his individualism:

> In the order of things established by God after the fall in order that the world might go on, man is in fact master of things; he can make a tower up to heaven of bricks baked in the fire and bitumen. He can also make a name for himself, for no natural obstacle keeps him from manifesting his pride to high heaven . . . Such is

5. Um, *Word of the Cross*, 16.

the city . . . To the desire in the creature for spiritual conquest corresponds a desire or order from the Creator, he who knows that man's spiritual conquest can only lead to one end—spiritual and material death . . . But because God wants his creature to live, he keeps the break from happening.[6]

This is the intimate dance between will and Will. The former is constantly embedded within and imbued by the latter. It is a source of utterly *incomprehensible* despair for the Almighty to witness its deviations and adulterations. Although death may sometimes seem like a preferable alternative to subjectively denigrated life, our death is *never* preferable to our dear Lord. We are all intimate parts of Him. Yet, if one continues to will his aberrant ways—and the Lord's lovingkindness fails to fully imbue his spirit—then the Father unfortunately has no choice but to take extreme measure.

Before rounding out the chapter, let's lighten the mood a bit and show an example of spirit-filled desire in action. For those of us used to driving to church in our leather-seated and pleasantly air-conditioned vehicles, the fact I'm about to share will leave a resounding impact upon your heart. I'd like to talk about a certain place of Christian worship deep in the Ethiopian highlands, a church called *Abuna Yemata Guh*.

Abuna Yemata Guh is a so-called monolithic church, carved into a *thousand-foot-high* sandstone cliff. This sandstone pillar lies atop the face of a relatively steep mountainside, making the church even more of a sight to behold.

Jean-Claude Latombe

6. Ellul, *Meaning of the City*, 16.

PART III: Foundations of a Living Word

The chapel itself lies near the tip-top of the rightmost sandstone formation, nestled up and around the back. Although this is an awe-inspiring sight to behold, it is right about now that the modern might say, "Yeah that's pretty crazy, but I'm sure they have stairs or something, right?" Hopefully, this was said out of the locals' earshot, because us first-world, modern folks have no idea how lucky (and insulated) we are!

Let's take a look at some parts of the journey to the chapel.

changyate/Chang's Adventures

Once locals have made the trek up the side of the near 45°-angled hill, it is time to scale the bottom of the sandstone face. Just before the churchgoers reach the sandstone, they jettison their shoes in order to maximize their grip on the rock. Luckily, this first portion of the trek is "only" 19 feet high; the *scary* part still looms ahead![7]

A good 15 to 30 minutes later, depending on how much of a cardio and adrenaline junky one is, one reaches an overlook.

---

7. See Bearak's, "Climbing to Ethiopia's Church in the Sky," The Washington Post.

LIFE IS THE GIFT

Atlas Obscura

This is no Yellowstone National Park-like, come-up-smile-snap-a-picture-and-lean-on-the-railing overlook . . . This is a place where man comes face to face with the intimate balance between life and death, as he gazes below at the valley floor, nearly *seven hundred feet* below him. The only restraint needed—God's Hand.

It is not too long after this sweat-inducing scene that the dedicated churchgoer finally reaches his destination—one of the most breathtaking chapel interiors known to man. It is at once intricate, quaint and pastoral, a harkening back to the days in which God was the most prominent concern of man.

Jean-Claude Latombe

PART III: Foundations of a Living Word

Abuna Yemata Guh is one of the last standing examples of the true dedication and submission of man to God; it stands as a stark reminder to the modern world of the bare *mortality* that we humans have here on earth. It reminds us of the awe-inspiring *dedication* believers can (and should) have to their Savior.

CHAPTER 11

BLACK AND WHITE

"Life is wasted if we do not grasp the glory of the cross, cherish it for the treasure that it is, and cleave to it as the highest price of every pleasure and the deepest comfort in every pain. What was once foolishness to us — a crucified God — must become our wisdom and our power and our only boast in this world."

—JOHN PIPER[1]

"So I say to you: Ask and it will be given to you; seek and you will find; knock and the door will be opened to you. For everyone who asks receives; the one who seeks finds; and to the one who knocks, the door will be opened."

—LUKE 11:9-10[2]

WE LIVE IN AN age of burgeoning moral relativism. Gender has proliferated into a "continuum," and the former acronym "LGB" has transformed into an ever-expanding "LGBTQ+." The opinion on hardcore drugs in many countries has gone mild (look at Amsterdam as an extreme example), and

---

1. Piper, *Don't Waste Your Life*, 9.
2. ESV.

there has been a recent softening towards pedophilia (look at California's recent laws related to age of consent).

The individualism created by Western civilization has insidiously snowballed into hedonism and self-righteous stoicism. And this undercurrent has now taken to the media and the airways, slithering from impressionable mind to impressionable mind. This is the flipside of "freedom." A concept that was once an outstanding intellectual beacon of steadfast spirituality and common sense has now warped into an antithetical of its former self.

Fortunately for us, there *is* an answer to all of this—the Word and the Savior, and all that these entail for our society. We cannot cling to egotistic "self-help" plans, and we must not seek a material way out for our society. We must learn to *submit* ourselves to the Lord. There are myriad forces within modern society—some of these even "religious" forces themselves—that are actively working *against* the spiritual integration of humanity.

For an example of such a force, we need look no further than the current pope, Pope Francis.

There's an article on *www.cathloic-sf.org* called "Pope calls for politics to rediscover its vocation to work for common good."[3] One might expect the Pope's message to emphasize God's Hand in politics and to redirect believers back to a role of reverence of and submission to the Lord. Alas, the Pope's words are anything but Spirit-infused and upward-looking. Pope Francis takes a decidedly *materialistic* view on the ills and issues of the modern world, urging folks to essentially just "go with the flow" and live in peace and harmony. His words sound far more like the lyrics of a famously secular Beatles song than words of the Lord.

Let's take a look at a collection of the Pope's quotes from the article:

- "If every human being possesses an inalienable dignity, if all people are my brothers and sisters, and if the world truly belongs to everyone, then it matters little whether my neighbor was born in my country or elsewhere."
- "Certain populist political regimes, as well as certain liberal economic approaches, maintain that an influx of migrants is to be prevented at all costs . . . One fails to realize that behind such statements, abstract and hard to support, great numbers of lives are at stake."

3. Wooden (2020).

- "Whereas individuals can help others in need, when they join together in initiating social processes of fraternity and justice for all, they enter the 'field of charity at its most vast, namely political charity.'"
- "[I]f someone helps an elderly person cross a river, that is a fine act of charity. The politician, on the other hand, builds a bridge, and that too is an act of charity but on a larger scale."

Perhaps if one were to consider these quotes out of their wider context, there would be no pressing spiritual issues. Unfortunately, when one realizes that—in making these ostensibly "even-handed" and "peace-harkening" statements—the Pope is actually *taking a political side*, things become rather frightening.

For example, when the first quotation is considered in sociopolitical context, it is an obvious reference to the issue of illegal immigration. This is a highly *partisanly divided* issue. The second quote is even more explicit, referring directly to Donald Trump and other so called "populists," while calling the principles of *nationalism* "abstract and hard to support."[4] The third quotation is simply an expansion upon the Pope's disdain for nationalistic principles, and the final quote hammers the nail in even deeper.

The trouble with all of this is that there is made to be a *false dichotomy*—heartless nationalism versus compassionate and Spirit-infused globalism. In order to grow ever closer to the ideal society in Christ, we must ditch such a narrow view of our political options.

To rid ourselves of such a false division, all we must do is meditate upon Matthew 6:10—"Your kingdom come, Your will be done, *on earth as it is in heaven*." The relevance is that there is a will to be carried out on this earth; this world is not a free-for-all, "waiting room" of a domain. The Pope would no doubt defend his position in light of this verse, perhaps delivering something like, "Yes, and that is exactly why we must treat all people on earth with the same Love that our Father would treat them in Heaven." Nonetheless, it is not exceedingly hard to see why this idealistic principle falls totally flat—God is not a nebulously flee-flowing and passive being. Rather, our God uses *structure, discipline,* and *reproach* when He needs to. By extension, it is our job to use these tools on earth as well.

The reason why nationalism seems closer to God's will on earth than does globalism is directly tied to God's aforementioned capacities of

---

4. No, Trump is no angel. And yes, he's a raging narcissist. But he does represent a somewhat refreshing departure from recent "establishment" candidates.

structure, discipline and reproach. The notion that God would want us to be unstructured and incapable of political discipline is absurd, and it does not mesh with scripture. The core reason why nationalism is closely aligned with His will is that the sociopolitical principles of *structure* and *discipline* trump all others.

An easy metaphor to use is that of raising a child and being a loving parent. If all the parents who were completely unable to provide discipline to their children simply pawned them off to parents who were able to provide said discipline, then we'd be in a very sorry spot. Wouldn't it be better if we could simply teach everyone to be a *better parent*, instead of having to shuttle the poor kids around? Stated in terms of immigration and nationalism: wouldn't it be better if we could simply teach and allow *every country* to *treat their citizens better*, instead of forcing the more structured and disciplined countries to bear the burden? Such a method of structure-guided governance meshes more tightly with the Word than does any sort of globalist scheme.

The whole debate on "nationalism versus globalism" is a mere symptom of the moral relativity of today's culture; we are so desperately afraid of absolutes. For many mathematicians, logicians and philosophers of modernity, the *paradox* that is "It is an absolute truth that there are no absolute truths" has completely flown over their heads. This lack of consideration of any sort of *fundamental truth* for our world has seeped into numerous nooks and crannies, causing cultural disaster after disaster.

For an intellectual example of the complete denial of truth, one need look no further than Richard Rorty and his philosophical musings. Though Rorty was no doubt a brilliantly talented man, he spun himself in conceptual circles around the main problem that consumed him—the nature of *Truth*. Here we see a brief explanation of his views from *Stanford Encyclopedia of Philosophy*:

> [Rorty's] point is that our ordinary uses of these notions always trade for their content and point on particular features of their varying contexts of application. His further point is that when we abstract away from these different contexts and practices, in search of general notions, we are left with pure abstract hypostatizations [or reifications] incapable of providing us with any guide to action at all. The upshot, Rorty holds, is that *we simply do not have a concept of objective reality* which can be invoked either to explain

the success of some set of norms of warrant, or to justify some set of standards over against others. (emphasis added)[5]

That last sentence is profoundly important.

In essence, Rorty's philosophy does not allow for any one True set of moral rules. It could even be said that his system does not even allow for any sort of simply true moral rules. Rorty's views are associated with what's called the "postmodernist" intellectual movement, a trend of thought which brings together numerous scholars from around the globe. The one thing these theorists have in common—an outright denial of *objectivity, morality* and *Truth*. No longer can us believers idly look on as this movement wriggles its way into the mainstream. Make no mistake: this intellectual undercurrent is a grave *spiritual danger*.

For all of Rorty and his fellow postmodernists' emphasis upon "pragmatism" and philosophical opportunism, it is interesting to see how the societal utility of Truth is roundly and willfully dismissed. It would be interesting to ask these folks one simple question—"would it not be of great pragmatic utility to at least *assume* the existence of a moral absolute, simply to give people some unified structure to work with and, at the very least, tinker on?"

To the postmodernists and other assorted Truth-deniers, the visceral fears involved with such subjects as moral absolutes, Truth, and God are too much to handle, psychologically speaking. Such issues are brushed aside and wishfully assumed to hold no theoretical or ethical weight. This is by no means something that invades only philosophy; this vein of thought has infiltrated the modern physics department and science departments at large.

Society is at a critical stage in which this toxic theoretical waste has the potential to seep down into the minds of the everyday man and woman. It is absolutely imperative that we anchor into our Absolute—God and Jesus Christ.

Although our Redeemer was sent to earth, although *it is finished*, we still have a black and white moral imperative. Even after the rigid legalism of the post-Moses world has faded away, there still exists *ethical absolute*. The choice is binary—spiritual redemption or no redemption; submission to the Lord or no submission; interface with the Spirit or no interface. It's really quite simple.

---

5. Ramberg, "Richard Rorty," para. 14.

PART III: Foundations of a Living Word

Let's imagine for a second a particularly moving scene. The Lord looks down from above and sees what society has become. He is dismayed and restless. He sees all the moral ambiguity, relativism and gray. But he is a proactive God. He reaches down and places two large, colored buttons for us to press; it's up to us and only us. There is a green one. "REDEMPTION" is written on it. And there is a red one, with "REJECTION" written on it.

Past the specifics, this is no hypothetical scenario. God has already done this, and we all have the *choice* to press whichever "button" we'd like. Which one will we choose?

PART IV

Coming in from the Rain (But Away from the Spirit)

CHAPTER 12

THE INTRODUCTION OF CUSHION

"The peculiar predicament of the present-day self surely came to pass as a consequence of the disappointment of the high expectations of the self as it entered the age of science and technology. Dazzled by the overwhelming credentials of science, the beauty and elegance of the scientific method, the triumph of modern medicine over physical ailments, and the technological transformation of the very world itself, the self finds itself in the end disappointed by the failure of science and technique in those very sectors of life which had been its main source of ordinary satisfaction in past ages."

—WALKER PERCY[1][EPI]

180 YEARS AGO, ANESTHESIA was first used to help a patient. Considering the timeline of the writing of the Bible—from roughly 1500 BC to roughly 95 AD—this invention is mind-bogglingly *recent*.

Only *two years* after anesthesia came into the world, the telegraph was born, the world's very first means of near-instant, cross-spatial communication. Between the birth of the telegraph and the year 1900, there were over thirty major inventions, from the passenger elevator, the burglar alarm and barbed wire to the typewriter, the telephone and the lightbulb.[2]

---

1. Percy, *Lost in the Cosmos*, 112–113.
2. For all history on technology, see McNeil, *History of Technology*.

PART IV: Coming in from the Rain (But Away from the Spirit)

In these days, man's soul was lit ablaze with *material* passion. His life's calling was to create and innovate. And create and innovate folks most certainly did, in abundance. The late nineteenth century was a mere stepping stone on the way to the massive material and social change the world experienced in the first half of the twentieth century. Whereas the innovations of the former age were grand in scientific scope, the inventions of the latter era were grand in *personal* and *domestic* ways. The inventions of the first half of the twentieth century found their way into man's own living room.

In 1902, air conditioning was born, and the next year the iconic Orville and Wilbur Wright became the world's first airplane pilots. A mere half decade after this, Henry Ford introduced his famous "Model T" vehicle. 1920 marked the beginning of commercial radio broadcasting, and 1927 marked the birth of the television, with the introduction of frozen foods in 1929.

To get a visual idea of just exactly how rapidly these domestic changes were happening, let's take a look at the design of the refrigerator throughout the decades:

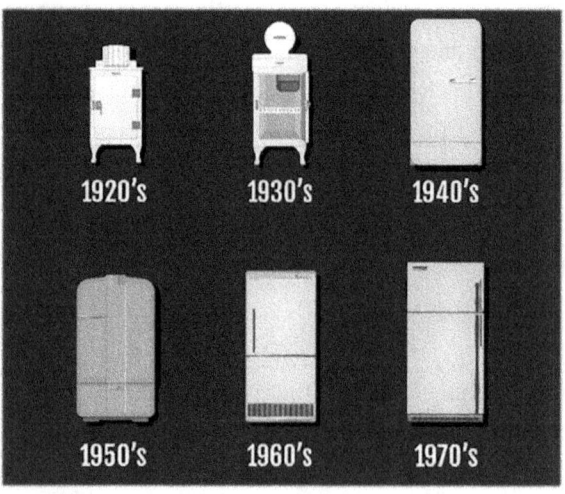

www.bigchill.com

In just two short decades, there was a stratospheric lift off in cooling technology and domestic aesthetics. In contrast, comparatively little has changed around the home from the year 2000 to 2020. This visual of the refinement of the fridge is just one tiny part of the sweeping process of innovation that took place in the twentieth century. Behind the aesthetic

The Introduction of Cushion

scenes, there was a far deeper bundle of *economic* and *social* changes sweeping the globe.

For a fair portion of the twentieth century, man's physical and mental industriousness rose in tandem with the physical and social changes around him. Throughout the first half of the twentieth century, the blue-collar man was a societal staple and lived an especially bare-knuckled sort of life. The second half of the century slowly snuffed out the blue-collar man, making of him, in many cases, an obedient office worker.

To get an idea of the environment the working-class man originally occupied and how this rapidly changed, we have the following excerpt from "The Age of Social Transformation" in *The Atlantic* by the late Peter Drucker:

> The workers of 1900—and even of 1913—received no pensions, no paid vacation, no overtime pay, no extra pay for Sunday or night work, no health or old-age insurance (except in Germany), no unemployment compensation (except, after 1911, in Britain); they had no job security whatever. Fifty years later, in the 1950s, industrial workers had become the largest single group in every developed country, and unionized industrial workers in mass-production industry (which was then dominant everywhere) had attained upper-middle-class income levels. They had extensive job security, pensions, long paid vacations, and comprehensive unemployment insurance or "lifetime employment."[3]

Here's something telling—in 1850 the average U.S. worker clocked 3,150 *to* 3,650 hours a year, while in 1987 the average worker clocked 1,949 hours a year.[4] In 2016, *The Wallstreet Journal* conducted a study on how the average American uses their free time, and the results are highly informative and interesting. The average U.S. worker spends nearly *three and a half hours* a day watching TV and/or consuming other media, and the average *unemployed* American spends nearly *seven hours* a day doing so.[5] Yet even these numbers don't paint the full picture.

We as a culture tend to view the "8-hour work day" as some sort of monolithic time period in which everybody is maniacally focused and immersed in their work, no matter how mind-numbing it may be. In social surveys even, this entire block of "work" is bundled into one category. In

---

3. Drucker, "Social Transformation," para. 15.
4. Schor, *The Overworked American*.
5. Light, "Leisure Trumps Learning."

PART IV: Coming in from the Rain (But Away from the Spirit)

these it isn't possible that one should have free time during this ostensibly "working" period. If such surveys were to ascertain what exactly was done during the work day, the average leisure time for Americans would skyrocket, perhaps up to ten to eleven or more hours a day in some cases. Unless one happens to be in one's field of unbridled passion and skill, it is exceedingly rare for one to find the highly sought-after state of "psychological flow" in today's work environments.

On the business and technology media site, *Thrive Global*, we see a telling assessment of the average modern workday. This article claims that per each eight-hour workday, the average worker is only productive for *two hours and 53 minutes* of it.[6] The article then cites a study in which anonymous full-time workers divulged how they spend their eight-hour days. Here's the rundown:

The most popular unproductive activities listed were:

1. Reading news websites–1 hour, 5 minutes
2. Checking social media–44 minutes
3. Discussing non-work-related things with co-workers–
4. Searching for new jobs–26 minutes
5. Taking smoke breaks–23 minutes
6. Making calls to partners or friends–18 minutes
7. Making hot drinks–17 minutes
8. Texting or instant messaging–14 minutes
9. Eating snacks–8 minutes
10. Making food in office–7 minutes[7]

I will be the first to admit that I am no stranger to this sort of routine, especially having worked in jobs that did nothing to challenge or stimulate me. This sort of schedule is symptomatic of our modern society as a whole. It could be said that the modern man *complains* more than all of his predecessors combined, all the while he has the most *comfortable* style of living yet known to the human race. The proliferating modern distractions, many of which are listed on the above list, have fooled us into thinking that we have "no time" and that we get "no breaks." Our consciousnesses are so

6. Curtin, "The Average Worker."
7. Curtin, "The Average Worker," 19–29.

The Introduction of Cushion

severely split that we cannot so much as genuinely enjoy a moment of idle time. We have this crushing urge to "be productive" and "useful." But this urge ends up driving us the opposite direction.

I certainly don't mean to say that the Word dismisses the fruits of leisure and rest. This would be profoundly untrue. I stress what the Bible says about the relationship between *work*, *will* and *submission to the Lord*. In Luke 12:47 we have, "And that servant who knew his master's will but did not get ready or act according to his will, will receive a severe beating,"[8] and then in 2 Corinthians 13:5 we have, "Examine yourselves, to see whether you are in the faith. Test yourselves. Or do you not realize this about yourselves, that Jesus Christ is in you?—unless indeed you fail to meet the test!"[9]

It is not our God's will that we remain overly idle and passive in our lives. The way we can "get ready" and "act according to [H]is [W]ill" is by doing just that: by being productive and working diligently at something through which we can show others the Word. In relation to the Corinthians verse, there is no other way to test ourselves than to put ourselves to work for a worthy cause, no matter how banal or boring this cause may seem at first.

But theologically speaking, things aren't that simple. In addition to the technological and social progresses of the early and mid-twentieth century, theology experienced the same intense growth pangs as did society at large. For an excellent discussion of the relationship between theology and society in the post-WWII period, we turn once more to Kate Bowler's *Blessed: A History of the American Prosperity Gospel*:

> The fear of extinction by nuclear weapons found its way into the school room where children practiced "Duck and Cover" drills and into popular culture . . . Even prosperity itself now seemed a menace: what was it doing to the children? School boards and universities produced a flood of social control films meant to tame this new generation who knew nothing of the work ethic and sacrifices of their parents and grandparents . . . The pleasant conformity of the age could not mask many Americans' vague and general unease. Was this all there is? . . . Observers dubbed the 1950s' moody mix of sun and clouds "The Age of Anxiety."[10]

---

8. ESV.

9. ESV.

10. Bowler, *Blessed* (Oxford Press version), 58.

PART IV: Coming in from the Rain (But Away from the Spirit)

This undercurrent of existential angst bred a strange fusion between materialism and spiritualism. Bowler goes on to mention:

> By the late 1960s, people spoke of "Jesus Freaks" and noted a wave of barefoot enthusiasts often armed with a 1966 New Testament translation called *Good News for Modern Man*. Tradition was out; authenticity was in. As one evangelist observed, "I don't know what; there's something happening. . . .But people . . . they're more interested in pentecostalism and the occult, mysticism, Buddhism, eastern religions. There's a tremendous interest in the unknown."[11]

What we see here is a sort of "mindful awakening," so to speak, as opposed to a spiritual one. As comforts grew and social norms and regulations grew laxer, man's mind was left yearning for *structure*. Alas, all structure that can be found outside the embrace of Jesus is that which leaves one longing for more substance.

On the other hand, not every route to Jesus is created equal. Salvation is Salvation; I don't mean to question that. What I mean to say is this— theological differences are not things to be ignored. Theology has an immeasurable impact on our personal relationships with Jesus, God and the Spirit.

I'll now introduce what I call a "theology of cushion," what seems to be the operating theology behind modern-day Christianity. This theology of cushion or TOC can be summarized like so:

> TOC: Although the Lord is our creator and sustainer, his role here on earth is to facilitate us and help us in our day-to-day, worldly actions and endeavors. The Lord has his domain—Heaven. And we have our domain—the earth. Although God does have some degree of control over this earth, our cultures and societies upon it ultimately shape who we are and how we come to God. Additionally, there is no reason to make great sacrifices for the Lord or undergo great acts of personal submission, simply because we live in the modern day, and we have moved beyond that sort of thing. Our job on earth is to achieve successes for ourselves, but also to keep God in mind as we achieve.

It is doubtful that anyone, when confronted, would fully agree with this bluntly stated theology. I truly hope nobody would. . . ! Rather, the "theology of cushion" is symbolic of our modern relationship with the Lord.

---

11. Bowler, *Blessed* (Oxford Press version), 70.

The Introduction of Cushion

To get an idea of what we need to do to move past this corrosive theology, we can look back to something written near the beginning of this book:

> First and foremost, we must strike a proper balance between (i) *individualism* and *collectivism* and (ii) *soul, spirit* and *Spirit*. After straightening out the above issues, we must find the middle ground between two extremes. On one end there is the prosperity gospel-like emphasis on the physical and on the other a Gnostic-like disdain for the physical realm. We must simultaneously find a way to restore the ancient emphasis on the community and on the Divine covenant. We must humble the modern man, without diminishing his connection to the Almighty.

The core reason TOC is woefully lopsided is because it places far too much emphasis on man's mind, as opposed to his soul or spirit. The TOC over-materializes the Divine and makes it seem as if the Lord is either (i) physically inert or unwilling to intervene in material matters or (ii) hyper-focused on man's material and physical circumstances. Spawning off from these two views, there are two main modern theological platforms.

The first platform corresponds to (i). According to this position, the Lord is either not inclined to intervene in the physical world or simply ill-equipped to do so. We see this variety of the "comfort gospel" in modern Catholicism, Lutheranism and Orthodox Christianity.

Then we have the platform corresponding to (ii). Here, God is hyper-focused on the material and physical, and we see the comfort gospel collide with the prosperity gospel, resulting in the theology of many modern Baptists, generalized Protestants and Pentecostals. There is not anything *intrinsically* wrong with any one of these denominations. Rather, they have been strongly impacted by modern society and its wildly changing whims.

CHAPTER 13

It's All Gray Now

"Accepting that the world is full of uncertainty and ambiguity does not and should not stop people from being pretty sure about a lot of things."
—Julian Baggini[1]

"Evangelicalism as a movement is rushing headlong toward theological ambiguity, which is another way of saying apostasy."
—Michael Horton[2]

I've already mentioned modern society's ongoing battle with moral ambiguity. What I haven't done is go into any sort of depth. We will now tackle head-on some of the most pressing moral issues of modernity. But before we get too deep, I should mention something, no matter how trivial it may seem—if we had all *agreed upon* a unified moral code, in addition to a higher, unified reality (God), there would be no reason to debate any of these issues that get us so heated and vicious. It is without the unity of God that we are heavily pitted against one another, believer versus believer.

---

1. Baggini, "What Is This?" para. 9.
2. Found in Balmer, *Encyclopedia of Evangelicalism*, 342.

It's All Gray Now

Let's start out with a concrete and contentious example. By terms of sheer principle, *abortion* should not even be a matter of debate. By raw Will, our Lord does not seek that *anyone* is to be murdered.

To get a grip on how morally ambiguous modern society has become, we will visit a comprehensive series of Gallup polls conducted on the topic of abortion.[3] Let's start off with a heavy-hitter: in 1993, a full 34 percent of Americans answered that "abortion should be legal in *all* circumstances." Just ten years later, the first continuous-use birth control pill was approved by the FDA. Moreover, in 1996 a full 56 percent of Americans described themselves as "pro-choice."

As is the case with any morally ambiguous issue, there has been much change in public opinion throughout the decades.

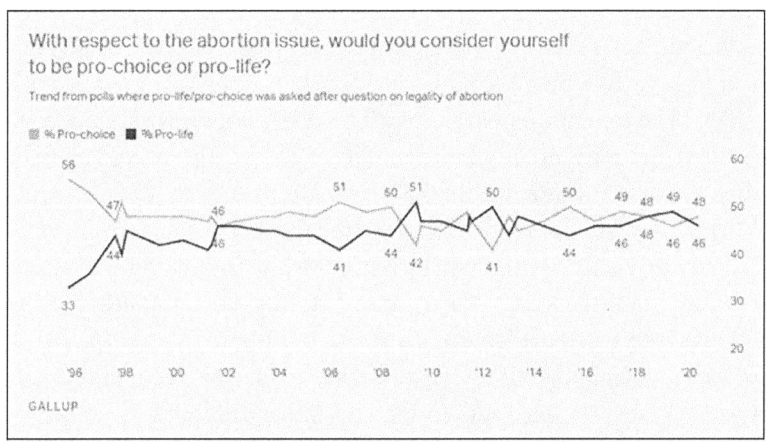

We are now locked in a moral tug of war. The pro-choicers belabor individualism and personal freedom, while the pro-lifers emphasize the sanctity of human life. Even more startling than this is the modern relationship between what's societally *feasible* and what's morally *permissible*. In other words, what's right "in principle" doesn't always turn out to be societally practical or humane and vice versa. For a perfect example of this dynamic at work, we can look at the distinction between different varieties of pro-choice and pro-life standpoints.

For starters, there are the two "hardliners," those who are pro-choice no matter what and those who are pro-life no matter what. Then, there are those who are pro-life with exceptions and those (though this is rarer) who

---

3. See https://news.gallup.com/poll/1576/abortion.aspx.

PART IV: Coming in from the Rain (But Away from the Spirit)

are pro-choice with some exceptions. This "with exceptions" standpoint on abortion, the "yeah, but. . . " one, is the most common.

According to Gallup, in 2020 29 percent of Americans think that abortion should be legal under any circumstances, 50 percent think that it should be legal under only some circumstances, and 20 percent think that it should be illegal in all cases.[4] This is a perfect example of the split between what's societally feasible and what's right based on moral principle. In terms of raw morality, abortion should *never* be allowed. A society where babies are *never* killed needs to be vehemently sought after. With all the moral ambiguity of modern society, abortion has gotten its feet in the door and beguiled the public into thinking that it is a "practical" and "humane" decision. At the very least, abortion must be seen as a very grave and extremely regretful thing.

If abortion is made to be a light and breezy decision, something that is meant to serve as a buffer for poor life decisions, then we have already lost the fight. The same principle exists with sin—although we are *all* sinners, we cannot and must not *normalize* sin. If we do, sin will abound more than it already does. This is a maxim that our society needs to heed. Maniacally obsessing over the "free choice" of the woman has done us little good.

Broadly speaking, the phenomenon of moral ambiguity falls under the heading of American "secularization," the insidious slithering of moral relativism into society at large. For stats on this trend, we can take a look at another set of Gallup polls on the matter. In 2019, 26 percent of Americans answered, "Not too religious" to the question, "Thinking of the way you personally celebrate Christmas, is it a strongly religious holiday, somewhat religious or not too religious?", while 32 percent answered "Somewhat religious" to the question.[5]

Contrast these stats with the fact that 70.6 percent of the U.S. population identifies as Christian.[6] If we assume that *almost all* Americans who answered either "Not too religious" or "Somewhat religious" as opposed to "Do not celebrate" are themselves Christians, we can conclude that somewhere around half of all Christians (or perhaps more) do *not* take the birth of their own Savior very seriously. This is very startling.

When the average person hears the term "secular," he or she might simply assume that it means the complete absence of religion, or that it is

4. See https://news.gallup.com/poll/1576/abortion.aspx.
5. See https://news.gallup.com/poll/1690/religion.aspx.
6. See https://news.gallup.com/poll/1690/religion.aspx.

something which only outright atheists or agnostics would support. This is not true. Christianity itself can most definitely catch secularism. And, indeed, in many denominations and areas around the globe, it already has. It is a sad age in which we live in where one can see the terms "secular theology" and "Christian atheism." The former notion we see defined as follows:

> Secular theology rejects the substance dualism of modern religion, the belief in two forms of reality required by the belief in heaven, hell, and the afterlife. Secular theology can accommodate a belief in God—as many nature religions do—but as residing in this world and not separately from it.[7]

According to this description, the secular theist is someone who believes that God is *material*. Although a belief in God is no doubt preferable to a complete lack of belief, such a view simply cannot be and is not founded in scripture. In fact, such a belief cannot be found in any ancient monotheistic religion at all, neither can it be found in many polytheistic religions. The closest comparison I can make in terms of the "secular theist" is that between him and the seventeenth- and eighteenth-century deist.

Deism rose in tandem with advances in thought that accompanied the Enlightenment era. The crux of deism is that God is simply "a divine watchmaker."[8] That is, he serves as the "prime mover" of the universe, yet he *does not intervene* in the motions of the working universe. To see how similar the deist and the so-called secular theist are let's take a look at the following diagram:

---

7. Excerpt from https://en.wikipedia.org/wiki/Secular_theology, para. 1. See Crockett, *Secular Theology* for an overview.

8. In modern times, we've seen this metaphor deteriorate even further. Take Richard Dawkins's book, *The Blind Watchmaker*, for instance.

PART IV: Coming in from the Rain (But Away from the Spirit)

DEISM	THEISM
Deism is the belief in the existence of a supreme being, specifically of a creator who does not intervene in the universe	Theism is the belief in the existence of a god or gods, specifically of a creator who intervenes in the universe
Believes that that God does not intervene in human affairs	Believes that that God intervenes in human affairs
Does not accept miracles or supernatural revelations	Accepts miracles or supernatural revelations
Often practiced by religious people	Appeals to people from both ends of the religious spectrum

Pediaa.com

    From this alone, we can see just how socially corrosive widespread deism could be. Deism takes the *personal* and *emotional* aspects out of religion entirely. Considering the previously given definition of "secular theism," we can see how it is barely a "theism" at all. According to the above attributes, secular theism is far more similar to deism than to theism proper. On the whole, the goal of secular groups is to make American religion *more deist* and *less theist*. Secularists seek to adulterate the personal and emotional aspects of religious belief, making the world a "safer" and "more rational" place to live.

    Let's talk a bit more about deism. We can start by noting that the deist *god* would be a very peculiar god, a god startlingly unconcerned with the procession of the universe. Deism removes the Lord from His creation, inserting a *barrier* between Him and His creation. In theism proper, all of God's creations are seen by Him, intimate parts of Him. While in deism, there is no such intimacy. An apt metaphor for deism is that of an absent father. The deist god created his child, but he continuously fails to have any part in his life. Even more, he has no desire to see his child at all. The deist theology is—at bedrock—a *demonic theology*. Make no mistake about this.

    Now back to the queue.

It's All Gray Now

In today's age, we are used to seeing such article names as "Religion Doesn't Make People More Moral, Study Finds" and "Letter: Atheists are more moral than religious conservatives." It is commonplace to see people try to strongarm their way out of moral certitude and their Lord's all-powerful Love. Atop the latter article, there's a picture showing two young atheists, one of whom is wearing a t-shirt that says, "There's probably no God/ Now stop worrying/And enjoy your life." The other person stands defiantly, holding a sign that says, "Hug an Atheist." Atheism is no fringe movement; 14.1 percent of the world's population identifies as "secular/nonreligious/agnostic/atheist."[9]

We are now at a point at which these secular forces are trying to make black and white out of their moral gray.

Lee Jin-man/AP

In the past year there have been numerous sightings of pride flags and BLM banners in the *public* classroom.[10] Those parents who have put up a fight have, by and large, been met with disagreement with their fundamental claim—that *political* symbols have no business in a place of what is supposed to be *objective* learning. Of course, the secular, liberal objection to the argument is that these symbols, in fact, *are* objective. The secularists claim that these symbols are objective on *moral* grounds.[11]

---

9. See Stewart's *Science and Religion in Dialogue* for this statistic and more like it. Original statistic is from a survey taken by the City University of New York in 2001.

10. See Helwig, "Teacher Sparks Controversy" for one instance of many.

11. This sort of stuff leads us into some thorny, philosophical territory. In Christ, it is a given that "black lives matter"; in Christ "all lives matter." My biggest issue with

PART IV: Coming in from the Rain (But Away from the Spirit)

The "Black Lives Matter" brand—and it *is* a brand—is a little over seven years old. The hashtag #BlackLivesMatter first appeared on social media in the wake of the infamous George Zimmerman trial in July of 2013.[12] BLM has hugged closely to the sporadic "racially charged" shooting incidents that have occurred between its inception and today. One interesting thing to examine is the nature of the group's support (and lack thereof). In July 2016, following the shooting of a group of fourteen Dallas police officers by a black man, Micah Xavier Johnson, BLM experienced a *freefall* in support. Below are the exact statistics:

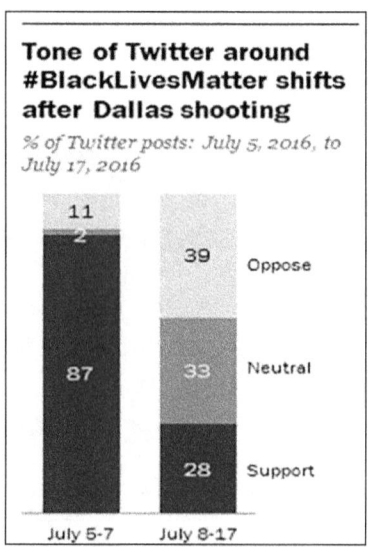

This trend ended up reversing completely in the next four years, culminating in our current moral morass in which 88 percent of all Democratic voters support the BLM brand and 45 percent of all white people support it as well.[13] It's interesting to note that BLM brand support correlates more with political ideology than with race, with 87 percent of all blacks

BLM is that it uses man-made *ideology* as a means to proclaim a "diagnosis" of American society. Another issue I have is the danger BLM invokes in terms of fundamental rights. BLM blurs the lines between racism on a *societal* level, or so-called systemic racism, and racism on a *personal* level. Legally speaking, the United States is *not* a racist country. All races are equal under the law; all can vote, all can marry, etc. On the personal level though, I'm sure there are plenty of racists. But what BLM fails to realize is that to "abolish racism" in a *personal* sense would amount to Orwellian thought crime.

12. Lebron, *The Making of BLM*.
13. See Thomas and Horowitz, "Support for BLM."

supporting the "cause" (compared to 88 percent of all Democratic voters).[14] Obviously, there are more Democratic voters in America than black folks, so we can see the partisan nature of things quite clearly. As it stands currently (as of September 2020) only 16 percent of Republican voters support the BLM brand.[15]

Enough with the stats. Let's see what exactly this "Black Lives Matter" group stands for. We'll begin by examining a highly peculiar document posted to the site *www.blacklivesmatter.com* called, "Healing in Action: A Toolkit for Black Lives Matter Healing Justice & Direct Action." The "toolkit" starts out with a set of questions:

> 1. How do we scaffold and support our well-being through direct action and confrontation?
> How do we begin to draw energy from naming and sourcing our visions more often than our wounds?[16]

"Scaffold and support our well-being". . . ? "How do we draw energy from naming and sourcing our visions". . . ? Excuse me? Quite obviously there is some strange current of New Age mysticism running through BLM's veins. And it is exceedingly bizarre to see it in action. Below these strange questions we see some even more startling sentences. Several pages below we see a header, "Grounding Exercises," and five different tasks below:

- Breathwork
- Box breath
- Body scan
- Chanting
- Check-ins[17]

And here's the descriptions given for the last two tasks:

> Chanting – Chanting and group singing are great ways to ground on a shared purpose or feeling. They are proven to regulate and sync up nervous systems within a group.
> Check-ins – Most folks make time for check-ins at the start of meetings. The magic of check-ins can only work in relation to

14. Thomas and Horowitz, "Support for BLM."
15. Thomas and Horowitz, "Support for BLM."
16. "Healing in Action," pg. 6.
17. "Healing in Action," pg. 5.

PART IV: Coming in from the Rain (But Away from the Spirit)

our vulnerability. Can we make room to ask each other how we are showing up and what we need to feel more present or grounded? What will you need during an action to stay grounded?[18]

Are we looking at a cult's mission statement or a BLM "toolkit?" The two are—for all intents and purposes—*indistinguishable*. Most importantly, there is a glaring lack of Truth, Jesus or God. New Age "spirituality" infused with Marxist-inspired principles of "social justice" is not a tasty recipe.

Below the "Grounding Exercises" header, we see the title, "Visioning" with the following description:

> Taking time to remember and re-affirm our vision is key to centering healing justice in our work. The reason why we fight is for a vision for ourselves, each other, and our communities where Black people are liberated. This visioning can continue to ground us in how we treat each other in our meetings, how we listen, and how we informally check in throughout the organizing process.[19]

Again, is this a cult ritual or an item in the BLM "toolkit?" The world may never know . . . What we *do* know are the statistics behind this New Age, bizarre moral "movement." As of June 2020, 67 percent of all Americans either "strongly support" or "somewhat support" it.[20] The big question is this—would they still support it if they knew exactly what it stood for? i.e., if they read this document and realized that BLM deals in New-Age mantra and cult-like, hocus pocus visualization and chanting. We can only hope and pray that the answer is *no*.

When secularization becomes the norm, the fundamental human need for *meaning* and *direction* does not magically evaporate. The human psyche can never be 100 percent secularized, and the BLM "toolkit" is a beautiful illustration of this principle. In the entire ten-page document, there is only one mention of God and no mention of Jesus. Moreover, the one mention of God in the document is of a highly secularized, nearly blasphemous New Age nature:

> Altar Building
> Altars exist in many cultures throughout the diaspora and a broad spectrum of traditions have unique altar building practices. If building an altar resonates with your culture and expression, an

---

18. "Healing in Action," pg. 5.
19. "Healing in Action," pg. 5.
20. Thomas and Horowitz, "Support for Black Lives Matter."

It's All Gray Now

altar can be a visual reminder of ancestors, Spirit, God or whatever we call that which is bigger than us. Altars can provide a place to reground and reconnect to our lineage and purpose. (emphasis added)[21]

Such a strange amalgamation of quasi-religious themes leads us to conclude that the BLM brand is situated in a sort of "spiritual anarchism," where anything and everything goes. The moral relativism that these people are trying so hard to disassociate from ends up crawling back into the picture. Although BLM claims to be fighting for some sort of objective morality, they end up blurring the lines on the back end. BLM juxtaposes "objective" morality with spiritual and motivational *relativism*. All the while, these folks forget that these two worldviews are glaringly incompatible.

Playing devil's (read: God's) advocate here, one can actually dissolve the BLM platform in a few leaps of fully "secular" argument. We could reason like so:

- If there is no cohesive basis of motivation or spirituality behind the "movement" then what is supporting this so-called objective morality? In other words, why exactly is it wrong that black people are being discriminated against? If there is no God to deem racism evil, then *why* is it evil?

- If you answer, "Because discriminating against people is a moral wrong" then you are making a grounded moral claim, an *absolute* judgement of morality. But, again, *through what means* are you making this claim? It's already established that you have no absolute spiritual grounding. So what are you basing your assertions on?

- If you were to say that "Discrimination is wrong because each person is morally equal by nature" then you would be appealing to an innate human quality. You would be presupposing a *fundamental* and *absolute* moral framework. If this is indeed the case, then why is there not also a fundamental spiritual and motivational framework to go along with it? Fundamental moral claims are *above* the level of science, so BLM cannot try to claim that "Well, science proves that we are all equal."

These are lapses of reasoning that demand answers.
Truly, it's all gray now.

---

21. "Healing in Action," pg. 6.

CHAPTER 14

Proverbs and Prosperity: Modern Theological Missteps

"I pity the man who praises God only when things go his way."
—Criss Jami[1]

"We are settling for a Christianity that revolves around catering to ourselves when the central message of Christianity is actually about abandoning ourselves."
—David Platt[2]

I'VE MENTIONED THAT BELIEVERS themselves aren't necessarily insulated from modern secularization. We've seen how secularization ultimately promotes moral and societal *relativism*. It advocates the toppling of any and all fundamental framework and inevitably leads to a corrosive emphasis on the *individual*, his pleasures and ambitions. What I have yet to fully discuss is the relationship between this secular trend and the modern Christian.

---

1. Jami, *Healology*, 35.
2. Platt, *Radical*, 7.

Proverbs and Prosperity: Modern Theological Missteps

Back in Chapter XI, "The Introduction of Cushion", I offered an overview of today's Christian theology, calling it "the theology of cushion" or "TOC" for short:

> TOC: Although the Lord is our creator and sustainer, his role here on earth is to facilitate us and help us in our day-to-day, worldly actions and endeavors. The Lord has his domain—Heaven. And we have our domain—the earth. Although God does have some degree of control over our earth, our cultures and societies upon this earth ultimately shape who we are and how we come to God. There is no reason to make great sacrifices for the Lord or undergo great acts of personal submission, simply because we live in the modern day, and we have moved beyond that sort of thing. Our job on earth is to achieve successes for ourselves, but also to keep God in mind as we achieve.

Although the TOC is not exclusively limited to the modern phenomenon of the "prosperity gospel," there is much overlap. To confirm this, we can begin by taking a look at the website of a certain prosperity preacher. I will decline to name this preacher's name out of respect.

On the sidebar of this preacher's site, there are eight main categories to choose from, ranging from "Finances" to "Life & Work". Under the Finances tab there are five different separate categories as well, "1. Believe," "2. Speak," "3. Pray," "4. Learn," and "5. Apply." Under the Apply category we see the mini article called "18 Bible Verses About Wealth and Prosperity." This article, whether it knows it or not, points straight toward the fundamental tenets of the prosperity gospel. Below are a few verses it features:

- Proverbs 22:7: Just as the rich rule the poor, so the borrower is servant to the lender.
- Proverbs 13:22: Good people leave an inheritance to their grandchildren, but the sinner's wealth passes to the godly.
- Proverbs 21:20: The wise have wealth and luxury, but fools spend whatever they get.
- Proverbs 3:9–10: Honor the Lord with your wealth and with the best part of everything you produce. Then he will fill your barns with grain, and your vats will overflow with good wine.

PART IV: Coming in from the Rain (But Away from the Spirit)

- Proverbs 10:22: The blessing of the Lord makes a person rich, and he adds no sorrow with it.[3]

When we examine the context of these verses and measure them against the prosperity message, we find that there is *misinterpretation* afoot. Before I "expose" what seems to be willful misinterpretation, let's lay all the verses out.

Proverbs 22:1 states, "A good name is more desirable than great riches; to be esteemed is better than silver or gold.", and 22:2 says, "Rich and poor have this in common: The Lord is the Maker of them all." And then, shortly after 22:7, in 22:9 we see, "The generous will themselves be blessed, for they share their food with the poor."

In order to wrap our heads around this little sleight of interpretational hand, let's show these interrelated verses side by side (we boldface the original verse found on the preacher's site):

- Proverbs 22:1 — "A good name is more desirable than great riches; to be esteemed is better than silver or gold."
- Proverbs 22:2 — "Rich and poor have this in common: The Lord is the Maker of them all."
- **Proverbs 22:7 — *"Just as the rich rule the poor, so the borrower is servant to the lender."***
- Proverbs 22:9 — "The generous will themselves be blessed, for they share their food with the poor."[4]

If we put the italicized verse next to 22:1 and 22:2, we begin to see that it almost seems out of place. Assuming that the Word is a cohesive whole—and given that, if all parts of it are indeed from Him, there is no word or verse that is truly "out of place"—it is *not* out of place. With this in mind, we can adjust our interpretation of 22:7 to fit neatly into the overall context of this portion of Proverbs. According to this preacher's interpretation, the Word here speaks about *material* riches and *material* "borrowing" and "lending." But, in the context of this area of the Bible, such an interpretation simply *does not fit*.

So what interpretation does fit here? Looking at 22:1, we see that a good name under the Lord is its own commodity. This is the one *invaluable*

---

3. Source cited in bibliography.
4. See bibliography.

commodity on this earth. This verse calls to mind 2 Corinthians 6:14, "Do not be unequally yoked with unbelievers. For what partnership has righteousness with lawlessness? Or what fellowship has light with darkness?" It is in this sense that the *spiritually* rich can be said to "rule" the *spiritually* poor.

What about the borrower and the lender then? We can use the exact same connotation as before, yielding—the *spiritual* borrower and the *spiritual* lender. The former is simply someone who receives spiritual warmth and kindness from somebody, while the latter is somebody who gives said kindness. The spiritual borrower is "servant" to the lender because the moral imperative is now on his/her shoulders to graciously accept the spiritual warmth and to spread it to others.

It is important that we fully contrast the two forms of interpretation—that used by the preacher in question and the one I just utilized. In the former interpretation, the *materially* rich rule over the *materially* poor. This interpretation flies in the face of numerous portions of the Word, perhaps the most prominent example being Proverbs 19:17, "Whoever is kind to the poor lends to the LORD, and he will reward them for what they have done." Nowhere in the Word does it say that the materially rich are *spiritually* dominant over the materially poor. This alone is enough to dismiss this preacher's interpretation. If we were to support this man's interpretation, we would be making our Lord into some sort of "might makes right" figure, and that is everything that He is *not*.

Assuredly, the preacher in question does not simply misinterpret just one verse. He misconstrues essentially every verse he uses in relation to finance and wealth. Although I cannot address all of the verses he uses, I can mention the next one in the lineup—Proverbs 13:22, "Proverbs 13:22: Good people leave an inheritance to their grandchildren, but the sinner's wealth passes to the godly." The preacher in question attempts to interpret "wealth" here as strictly *material* wealth. Yet, once again, when we look at the scriptural context in which this verse is situated, we can see how inaccurate such an interpretation is.

Let's see the logic here ... In Proverbs 13:21, we see "Trouble pursues the sinner, but the righteous are rewarded with good things." Clearly, *material* trouble does not always pursue the sinner. There is an abundance of *materially* rich yet *spiritually* impoverished men. Thus, if the first portion of the verse refers to spiritual trouble, then so must the last portion. Remember, back in Proverbs 13:7 we have the emphasis explicitly placed on

PART IV: Coming in from the Rain (But Away from the Spirit)

spiritual wealth: "One person pretends to be rich, yet has nothing; another pretends to be poor, yet has great wealth."

So how can 13:21, "[Spiritual] Trouble pursues the sinner, but the righteous are [spiritually] rewarded with good things." be meshed together with our preacher's view of 13:22? Let's see them side by side:

- 13:21 Spiritual Emphasis: "[Spiritual] Trouble pursues the sinner, but the righteous are [spiritually] rewarded with good things."
- 13:22 Prosperity Interpretation: "Good people leave a [material] inheritance to their grandchildren, but the sinner's [material] wealth passes to the godly.

I must admit, this preacher does get some things right. After all, if he didn't, he would have no platform to preach on! For 13:22, it is clearly the case that the sinner's *material* wealth passes to the godly. What other form of wealth could the sinner possibly have? What sense does it make that "Good people leave a [material] inheritance to their grandchildren. . . " though? As it so happens, not much at all.

Let's cut even deeper now and address some of the literary structure of these verses.

Verses 13:21 and 13:22 form a literary structure known as *chiasmus*. Chiasmus is Latin for "crossing," and it entails that certain parts of sentences (whether semantic or syntactic parts) are switched around for rhetorical effect. For example, "By day the frolic, and the dance by night."

13:21 and 13:22 form no ordinary chiasmus. This is a type of cross-sentential chiasmus, and it is simultaneously subtle and profound. For 13:21, we see an inversion of the normal associations of "trouble" and "reward"; these two terms are translated into spiritual terms. And then, in 13:22, according to the chiasmus structure, we see an inversion of the normal associations of "inheritance" and the "passing of wealth."

This chiasmus structure sticks with the overall theme of this area of Proverbs. Take for example 13:7, "One person pretends to be rich, yet has nothing; another pretends to be poor, yet has great wealth." as well as 13:12, "Hope deferred makes the heart sick, but a longing fulfilled is a tree of life." Both of these verses exhibit the very same inversion of normal semantic association. In the former, "being rich" is translated into spiritual terms just as "pretending" is cast in a new light. In the latter, "hope" is counterintuitively translated into materialistic terms just as "longing" is paradoxically

Proverbs and Prosperity: Modern Theological Missteps

cast into spiritual terms. This part of Proverbs—and even much of Proverbs entirely—is a beautiful expose of chiasmus in spiritual action.

Back to those two verses and their interpretations:

- 13:21 Spiritual Emphasis: "[Spiritual] Trouble pursues the sinner, but the righteous are [spiritually] rewarded with good things."
- 13:22 Prosperity Interpretation: "Good people leave a [material] inheritance to their grandchildren, but the sinner's [material] wealth passes to the godly.

What does the context of chiasmus in Proverbs tell us about the nature of 13:22? Well, it tells us that "inheritance" must be cast in a counterintuitive light; inheritance must be set in the *spiritual*! Thus, the context-fitting interpretation of the verse becomes this:

- "Good people leave a [spiritual] inheritance to their grandchildren, but the sinner's [material] wealth passes to the godly.

According to the context of the surrounding area of Proverbs (even Proverbs as a whole), this is the proper interpretation.

Although I've pointed out a theological misstep of a certain pastor, my goal is not to heap condemnation upon my fellow believers. I stand in spiritual solidarity with them in this age of growing spiritual chaos. After all, any sort of (genuine) believer is better than an outright atheist. Moreover, the pastor in question does orient the modern believer in the right way in many aspects. Our job here is to guide believers to a middle ground, between the ego-centric danger zone of high-flying prosperity gospel and the inert and lifeless bowing of the head found in traditional denominations.

Some may take offense that I have stooped so low as to "judge" a fellow believer and his scriptural interpretations. Yet, to claim as much would be a fundamental misinterpretation of what exactly "judgement" means. Below we see the most popular example that comes to mind when the believer thinks of judgement (Matthew 7):

PART IV: Coming in from the Rain (But Away from the Spirit)

> ³ "Why do you look at the speck of sawdust in your brother's eye and pay no attention to the plank in your own eye? ⁴ How can you say to your brother, 'Let me take the speck out of your eye,' when all the time there is a plank in your own eye? ⁵ You hypocrite, first take the plank out of your own eye, and then you will see clearly to remove the speck from your brother's eye.

This is a paradigmatic example of Biblical "judgement"—a reproach or an evaluation of someone else's *personal* state of being without adequate reflection upon one's own state of personal being.

If the other person were doing something *dangerous* to his brothers and sisters—say, brandishing a knife and screaming bloody murder—it would no longer be "judgement" for a brother or sister to step in and control the situation. This is the crux of the issue of judgement—if the behavior that is being judged crosses the line from harmless to explicitly harmful, then it is no longer termed "judging" if the person observing such behavior intervenes. In intervening in such a dangerous situation, one needn't pass *personal* blame or condemnation upon the person involved.

It is one thing to tell a person that he's an irredeemable demon destined for hell. It is another thing entirely to merely address or act upon his behavior without personal condemnation. Let's now take a look at two crucial verses on the topic of judgement (John 7:24 and 1 Thessalonians: 5:19–22):

John 7:24   New International Version

> ²⁴ Stop judging by mere appearances, but instead judge correctly."

> ¹⁹ Do not quench the Spirit. ²⁰ Do not treat prophecies with contempt ²¹ but test them all; hold on to what is good, ²² reject every kind of evil.

These two verses distill for us an ancient wisdom—prophecies and theologies are to be *tested*. They are to be *assayed*. Once we become believers and acknowledge the power of the Word, we should begin to desire

Proverbs and Prosperity: Modern Theological Missteps

Truth in all forms. One form of Truth happens to be theological and interpretational in nature. If God's Word is distorted, then all who read it miss out on the wisdom to be found in the True interpretation of it. Certainly, no one man or even one congregation or denomination can claim to hold this "True interpretation." Nonetheless, there are some points at which we can glimpse the faint outlines of this ultimate interpretation. And, if any one of us glimpses this penumbra, the spiritual burden is upon us to share it with our brothers and sisters. This is our mission.

Looking back on our proposed modern "theology of cushion" or TOC, we can see that it's certainly not just the pastor in question who has fallen into such a materialistic manner of thinking. In the context of prosperity, we must continually remind ourselves that it's all about the spiritual. Our earthly mind, heart, and material possessions are *secondary*.

CHAPTER 15

JESUS THE LIFE COACH

ON THE GOSPEL COALITION'S website *www.thegospelcoalition.org* there's a relatively recent article in the Christian Living section called "How Self-Help Can Become Self-Hurt." Here's the opening paragraph:

> I recently got an email from a self-help guru offering to help me be the architect of my life. Its message was much like you'd see in the self-help section these days: if you'll just do this or that, your life will be rich and full, and you'll get your act together. Plan it out, budget your time, and optimize your life.[1]

This article cuts to the core of the modern self-help paradigm—it offers an easy and ego-centered fix to the downtrodden and distracted. The article then moves on to address five core conceptual issues with self-help:

1. It is often prayerless.
2. It doesn't account for [mercurial] reality.
3. It focuses on the self.
4. It wrongly assumes I have the ability to change myself.
5. It puts the onus on us to shepherd ourselves.[2]

---

1. Larson, "Self-Help Can Become Self-Hurt," para. 1.
2. Larson, "Self-Help Can Become Self-Hurt," para. 7–10.

Short and sweet—self-help heaps an unfair burden upon man. He alone is supposed to be responsible for his mood, motivation, success and fulfillment. When one attempts to singlehandedly bear these burdens, one can often lose all motivation altogether. Moreover, even if one doesn't lose his motivation to achieve, he will surely lose all senses of meaning *beyond himself* and his own pleasure.

The author of the article then goes on to recount more of his personal encounter with self-help strategy:

> When I was writing my first book, I bought into self-help in a big way. In fact, that's how I got on the self-help guru's email list. As I was sitting in my bedroom, reading a well-thought-out action plan for building my audience, I was inspired and hopeful ... I pictured the book signings and the lines of people who wanted to buy the book. I just needed to follow the plan.
>
> But it didn't work. I followed the plan but found it slow going. Apparently, launching a book as an obscure author is not a recipe for success, and overcoming obscurity is a *long, slow, humbling process*. You can refresh your social media pages all you want, but you can't make people connect. (emphasis added)[3]

This little anecdote highlights one of self-help's fatal flaws—it can turn one into a demanding, impatient and self-centered human being. As we saw earlier, there really is no such thing as a through and through "secular" human. As much as man claims that he doesn't need a higher power in his life, his psyche still desperately craves a higher form of *meaning*. In this increasingly secular age, the lowbrow, junk food for the ego that is self-help is increasingly enticing to the wayward and fractured conscious.

A perfect example of the modern self-help mantra can be seen in the book, *You Are a Badass: How to Stop Doubting Your Greatness and Start Living an Awesome Life* (2013) from the "success coach," Jen Sincero. The second chapter of the book is entitled, "The G Word," and it dives straight into the conflict between Christianity proper and tepid and "free flowing" spirituality.

> I was so broke and clueless and sick of being such a weenie about really going for it in my life, that I was open for suggestions ... *Then I noticed how much better it made me feel* ... Then I became obsessed with it. Then *I started loving it*. Wherever you happen to stand on the God issue, let me just say that that this whole

---

3. Larson, "How Self-Help Can Become Self-Hurt," para. 12.

PART IV: Coming in from the Rain (But Away from the Spirit)

improving your life thing is going to be a lot easier if you have an open mind about it. *Call it whatever you want—* God, Goddess, The Big Guy, The Universe, Source Energy, Higher Power, The Grand Poobah, gut, intuition, Spirit, The Force, The Zone, The Lord, The Vortex, The Mother Lode—*it doesn't matter.* (emphasis added)[4]

Notice the emphasis here . . . It's all about "I"; Then *I* noticed how much better it made *me* feel . . . Then *I* started loving it, etc. God is reduced to a tool of ego massage, and this is a supreme act of blasphemy. To call the Lord by any myriad of names is to debase His value as the ruler and creator of the cosmos. This is not a "call it whatever you want" religion that us Christians have. This is black and white. God and Jesus. King and Savior.

To put this in more perspective, let's consider this in conjunction with the famous Sermon on the Mount.

He said:

3 "Blessed are the poor in spirit,
for theirs is the kingdom of heaven.
4 Blessed are those who mourn,
for they will be comforted.
5 Blessed are the meek,
for they will inherit the earth.
6 Blessed are those who hunger and thirst for righteousness,
for they will be filled.
7 Blessed are the merciful,
for they will be shown mercy.
8 Blessed are the pure in heart,
for they will see God.
9 Blessed are the peacemakers,
for they will be called children of God.
10 Blessed are those who are persecuted because of righteousness,
for theirs is the kingdom of heaven.

Now let's juxtaposition these Holy words with some of the juicy tidbits of self-help wisdom found in *You Are a Badass*. In Chapter 6 of this book, we see nine magical tips and tricks: 1. Appreciate how special you are, 2.

---

4. Sincero, *You Are a Badass*, 29.

Drown yourself in affirmations, 3. Do things you love, 4. Find a [mental] replacement, 5. Ditch the self-deprecating humor, 6. Let the love in, 7. Don't compare yourself to others, 8. Forgive yourself, and 9. Love yourself.[5]

Can you imagine how ridiculous our Savior would have sounded had he based his sermon around these nine "principles"? Let's see if I can illustrate:

> He said:
> Rise up all of you awesome people,
> You must empower yourselves.
> Great power lives within you,
> and you must appreciate how special you are.
> You are all so incredible,
> thus do all things you love,
> with no constraint and little restraint.
> For once you set yourselves free from self-doubt,
> you will come to see your greatness.
> So then, take my God's name into your hands,
> and call upon him when you need.
> For he is your personal motivator,
> and he is everything you could ever need.

Let that sink in for a bit . . . This is the exact sort of Jesus the modern secular, self-help-infused spirituality is advocating for. This is their dream. Such a Jesus would be stripped of his deity. He would be reduced to material-success-seeking public speaker. Enter Jesus the life coach.

In terms of our modern culture at large, this little illustration is just the "spiritual," relativistic side of things. Such tampering with Jesus's fundamental identity has insidiously crept into Christian theology itself, with the infamous "little gods theology" as prime example. The little gods theology is most prominently associated with the "Word of Faith" Evangelic movement, which is centered on the power of man's spoken word.

The theological results of the "Word of Faith" movement can be found in Kenneth Hagin's *The God-Kind of Life* (1989), in which he states that the believer is "called Christ" because "that's who we are, we're Christ!" Emphatically, we mere humans are *not* Christ. Such a viewpoint is borderline *heretical*.

Once "spiritual" folks and believers begin to see Christ in a merely *pragmatic* light, the implications for society as a whole are extremely

---

5. Sincero, *You Are a Badass*, 55.

PART IV: Coming in from the Rain (But Away from the Spirit)

corrosive. Where the Savior is debased to the level of life coach, society no longer has any overarching moral framework. All will inevitably collapse into relativism. This is no exaggeration.

CHAPTER 16

MACHIAVELLI WAS A CHRISTIAN

"How we live is so different from how we ought to live that he who studies what ought to be done rather than what is done will learn the way to his downfall rather than to his preservation."
—NICCOLÒ MACHIAVELLI[1]

NICCOLÒ MACHIAVELLI WAS A fifteenth-century Italian head of state, philosopher and writer. He is most popular for his work, *The Prince*, a work of highflying, grandiose political philosophy. To get an idea of what kind of man Machiavelli was, we can browse some quotes from *The Prince*:

- "If an injury has to be done to a man it should be so severe that his vengeance need not be feared."
- "[I]t is much safer to be feared than loved because... love is preserved by the link of obligation which, owing to the baseness of men, is broken at every opportunity for their advantage; but fear preserves you by a dread of punishment which never fails."
- "A prudent man should always follow in the path trodden by great men and imitate those who are most excellent, so that if he does not attain to their greatness, at any rate he will get some tinge of it."

1. Machiavelli, *The Prince*, 56.

PART IV: Coming in from the Rain (But Away from the Spirit)

- "Any man who tries to be good all the time is bound to come to ruin among the great number who are not good. Hence a prince who wants to keep his authority must learn how not to be good, and use that knowledge, or refrain from using it, as necessity requires."

For those of us familiar with "stoicism"—which I actually mentioned several chapters ago—these quotes should sound familiar. Alas, Machiavelli's philosophy is even more dangerous than mere stoicism. Machiavelli's thought advocates a society in which "might makes right," in which the most powerful party is always the rightful victor. Today, the whole "might makes right" worldview isn't active in the physical realm (in America, at least). We don't see people of power *physically* domineering those of lesser might. What we do see, however, is a more subtle, "white-collar" form of domination. And the most overt domain where this occurs is in the modern corporation, with the CEO exerting abstract power over his subordinates and the citizens of America at large.

Monash University in Australia has an interesting business blog called Impact. One of the most recent articles on Impact is called "Why Wicked CEOs Prevail: Dark Personality Traits of the Executive Suit." At the bottom of the article we see the section, "Corporate chameleons," detailing how bosses with psychopathic and narcissistic traits are able to woo their colleagues with such great facility.

> Fortune 100 companies such as Zappos adopt innovative and unorthodox methods such as 'The social test', 'Nice guy', 'The service test', and 'The ultimate test' to screen for candidates that best 'fit the organisation'. Narcissists tend to excel at these types of tests, making a favourable first impression and displaying a range of adaptable behaviours. These attributes help them to portray themselves as the 'best fit' for the organisation's needs, whatever that fit might be at that time. Studies show that leaders with high psychopathic attributes are also seen as more charismatic. This enables these leaders to manipulate and influence others. The superficial charm of wicked bosses smooths out awkward behavioural issues they might face.[2]

It is a sad fact of modernity that such "dark traits" as psychopathy, narcissism and egocentrism have become increasingly hard to spot. In ancient days, if your king was a raging psychopath, the proof was in the pudding

---

2. Monash Business School, "Why Wicked CEOs Prevail," para. 26–30.

with the guillotine and sword. In modern days, if your CEO is a raging psychopath, you might not be able to tell until it's too late.

With these facts in hand, we can touch on a very important modern issue: politicians. In the past half-decade there has been much uproar over this country's politicians. Nearly half of our country decries our current president (as of 2020) as a "fascist" and a "dictator," while the other half applauds his candor and bravery. Amongst us believers, the stats and divisions are similar. Some denominations are vehemently against President Trump's personal characteristics and supposed values, and others stand in adamant support. How exactly does this work?

The largely liberal news site, *The Atlantic*, released a piece addressing these divisions (and imparting much of its own bias) back in July of 2019. "The Deepening Crisis in Evangelical Christianity" stands boldly with the subtitle, "Support for Trump comes at a high cost for Christian witness."[3]

The article opens by displaying some of the deep convictions that Evangelicals (amongst other Christians) have for Trump:

> The rallygoers [believe] that Trump's era "is spiritually driven." When I asked whether he meant by this that Trump's supporters believe God's hand is on Trump, this moment and at the election—that Donald Trump is God's man, in effect—he told me, "Yes—a number of people said they believe there is no other way to explain his victories. Starting with the election and continuing with the conclusion of the Mueller report. Many said God has chosen him and is protecting him."[4]

This concession is short-lived as the article quickly moves to defensive. After citing the powerful stat that "from July 2018 to January 2019, 70 percent of white evangelicals who attend church at least once a week approved of Trump," the article calls the judgement of the modern Evangelical into question.

> The enthusiastic, uncritical embrace of President Trump by white evangelicals is among the most mind-blowing developments of the Trump era. How can a group that for decades—and especially during the Bill Clinton presidency—insisted that character counts and that personal integrity is an essential component of presidential leadership not only turn a blind eye to the ethical and

3. Wehner, "The Deepening Crisis."
4. Wehner, "The Deeping Crisis," para. 4.

PART IV: Coming in from the Rain (But Away from the Spirit)

moral transgressions of Donald Trump, but also constantly defend him?[5]

In other words, Trump is so blatantly a bad guy that how can anybody who claims to be "righteous" and "moral" not see that? This is *pathos* appeal at its finest. But it doesn't stand the test of rational thought.

Let's think about this in conjunction with some of the points I brought up about CEOs and dark personality traits. As I mentioned above, much has changed since the days of Niccolò Machiavelli. No longer are the characteristic traits of said dark psychology—self-centeredness, impulsivity, arrogance, etc.—on *overt* physical display. In the modern day, it has become increasingly easy for the psychopath to lurk beneath a charming "politician's smile." What this means for modern media is this: those who come across as slick and polished humanitarians can very well be psychopathic maniacs, and those who come across as abrasive and abrupt can very well be genuine and upright.

One of the biggest reasons why Donald Trump was elected is that he does not speak like a polished and pandering politician. Trump speaks plainly and bluntly to the common man of America. It is the hypocrisy and optical illusions of today's political establishment that have worn Americans weary. And we as believers, having tapped into the source of all things Good and True, are usually quite adept at seeing through pretense.

A perfect example of the modern-day Machiavellian is someone like Bill Clinton, or perhaps even his wife, Hillary.[6] These folks are smooth-talking, wide-smiling politicians, and they can certainly affect sincere emotion and motivation. Considering the elements of Machiavelli's philosophy, we can see how pandering and phoniness are parts of a calculated and rational strategy for personal gain. It is extremely doubtful that a modern-day Niccolò Machiavelli would advise global leaders to display *overt* violence or vengeful sentiment. He would likely advocate for the same approach that so many of today's greatest political panderers have taken. It's far less work this way. And, as it turns out, the modern man isn't too hard to fool.

Spiritual Machiavellianism is much more insidious, though it is certainly just as prevalent. In the modern phenomena of prosperity theology and "little gods" theology, we see Machiavellianism feature in prominently. We can glimpse spiritual Machiavellianism in the sermons of a certain

---

5. Wehner, "The Deeping Crisis," para. 6.

6. In case this gives off too strong a partisan bias, I should mention that George Bush wasn't too savory a character either.

Apostolic Pentecostal preacher. In one of his sermons, "I Shall Prosper," this pastor said the following:

> [God] said that "Whatsoever he doeth shall prosper."
> And that's where I'm trying to move to in my walk with God.
> I'm trying to get to the place, where *everything* I do,
> according to the Word and will of God,
> it comes to fruition.
> It's got to prosper.
> It's got to come to pass . . .
> I'm trying to get to the place, where *everything I touch*
> it *turns to gold*. (emphasis added)[7]

Machiavelli was a conqueror. Above all, he was a man who made things work for *him*. In the Machiavellian philosophy, there is no such thing as politely asking for power or success. But these sentiments fly squarely in the face of scripture. James 4:10 and 1 Peter 5:6 both express the crucial spiritual insight—"*Humble yourselves* before the Lord, and He will exalt you." (emphasis added)[8] In such pleadings to God as this pastor's sermon, we don't see self-effacement. We see man egocentrically attempting to take the power of the Spirit into his own hands, for *his* own means.

To round this all out, we can take another look at Michael Horton's brilliant book, *Justification* (2018). Horton illustrates how the modern cultural milieu is conducive to egotism and Machiavellian-like behavior.

> Drawing on this example, sociologist Steve Bruce explains, "Individualism, egalitarianism, liberal democracy, and science and technology all contribute to a general sense of self-importance, of freedom from fate." Consequently, "In the world of the mainstream churches and in the cultic milieu of alternative spirituality people are now generally unwilling to subordinate themselves to an external authority."[9]

This hits the nail squarely on the head. Modernity is the age of "me," the time of "I." We live in a world divorced from the bare living of our ancestors, a world removed from harsh physical realities and consequences. These facts have carried over into the spiritual realm of today. Even though

---

7. Taken from Bowler, *Blessed* (Oxford Press version), 117. Out of respect for the preacher in question, we will place the main source only in the bibliography.

8. ESV.

9. Horton, *Justification*, 19.

PART IV: Coming in from the Rain (But Away from the Spirit)

we've attained such material "success," there are many ancient boons of life that we will never experience.

Humble wooden edifices have morphed into shiny glass and steel megachurches. The once bucolic and idyllic walk to the altar has transformed into a bustling and hectic commute. With all these faux stressors and material privileges, it is quite easy for us to fashion religion into a quick and easy contraption for material comfort. However, we must lift our eyes upwards towards Him and resist.

Let it be said that Machiavelli—and everything he stood for—was not of God.

CHAPTER 17

Spiritual Procrastination

"The problem with spiritual procrastination is the uncertain time of the deadline."

—Kevin Thoman

Back in Chapter IV, "God's Man," I brought up something I called "ADHD of the spirit." I made a division between ADHD as it is currently diagnosed and the more penetrating and insidious variety that is spiritual ADHD. In setting up this term, I drew upon the insights mentioned in Chapter I, "Different Minds" by the anthropologist Jean Gebser in his *magnum opus*, *The Ever-Present Origin*.

In the first chapter, I utilized Gebser's distinction between "archaic consciousness" and "mythical consciousness." The former mode of mind was one of complete unity of mind and interconnection, while the latter was one of fracture and newfound division. I compared the transition from the former to the latter to the fall of man from the Garden of Eden. For all intents and purposes, this comparison serves us marvelously well.

Just to get a little refresher on the nature of Gebser's two forms of consciousness, we'll take another look at one of his beautiful explanations:

> The more man released himself from the whole, becoming "conscious" of himself, the more he began to be an individual, a unity not yet able to recognize the world as a whole, but only the details

PART IV: Coming in from the Rain (But Away from the Spirit)

(or "points") which reach his still sleep-like consciousness and in turn stand for the whole. Hence the magic world is also a world of pars pro toto, in which the part can and does stand for the whole. Magic man's reality, his system of associations, are these individual objects, deeds, or events separated from one another like points in the over-all unity.[1]

With this point of view in hand, we can go back to our notion of ADHD of the spirit. Such a malady of attention intersects with essentially every aspect of modern man's environment. It isn't too hard to see how the traits of Gebser's mythical consciousness describe the modern mind across numerous dimensions. Our focus is diverted into numerous tributaries—from the quick-hit highs of social media and gaming to the ubiquitous deluge of meaningless advertisement—and it is extremely tough to fight against the current.

One of the first symptoms that will pop up when one types in "ADHD" on the web is *procrastination*. Where ADHD is a malorientation of focus and where focus is the key ingredient in the completion of tasks, procrastination is an inevitable result. When it comes to ADHD of the spirit and spiritual procrastination, it is tempting to think a little too straightforwardly. We might be tempted to think, "Well . . . As long as you're going to church, you're focused on God." Alas, this is far from the truth.

Spiritual procrastination—just as mental procrastination—can take many forms. Just as one can be focused yet not focused on the *proper* things, one can be spiritually focused but lack overall spiritual orientation. Subtleties aside, the most defining feature of spiritual procrastination is this—deep down, man knows what he is doing (and not doing).

There is an article on the psychology news site Verywell Mind entitled, "The Relationship Between ADHD and Chronic Procrastination."[2] This article gives us six main themes when it comes to ADHD and procrastination: (i) Problems Getting Started, (ii) Getting Sidetracked, (iii) Last-Minute Propulsion, (iv) A Sense of Paralysis and Feeling Overwhelmed, (v) Impaired Sense of Time, and (vi) Fear of Failure. Each of these themes applies just as well to spiritual procrastination.

---

1. Gebser, *Ever-Present Origin*. Taken from Mohrhoff's "Evolution of Consciousness According to Jean Gebser," 54.
2. Low, "ADHD and Chronic Procrastination."

Spiritual Procrastination

PROBLEMS GETTING STARTED

"Give your life to God," "Give your life to Christ," "Ask Jesus into your heart," "Baptize yourself in the Holy Spirit." There are myriad terms and phrases thrown out into today's religious landscape. And if one takes all of this terminology too seriously, he or she is doomed to be trapped in spiritual indecision. All of this formality and social gravity can be enough to scare off even the most genuine of prospective believers. Many of us love to point out the pitfalls of the Pharisees' legalism and rigidity, but we casually overlook the implicit legalism thriving in the modern church.

There is a dual-fronted attack on the modern prospective believer. On one side looms legalistic self-centeredness and denomination-obsessed modern theology. On the other side the modern person's fractured and distracted consciousness threatens to undermine genuine religious experience in all aspects.

As Paul tells us in Romans, it is circumcision of the *heart* that the Lord lovingly looks upon and can thus sanctify the possessor of this heart through Christ Jesus.[3] The proliferation of modern cultural rites to Jesus, this is a growth of mere *social* circumcisions, less painful versions of what Abraham and his kin so faithfully underwent in the ancient days. By just saying, "I give my life to God" or "I ask Jesus into my heart" one does not circumcise one's heart. In order to do so, one must commune with the Savior and the Almighty, *heart-to-Heart*. One can *choose* to say such phrases while communing with Jesus and the Lord, but there is no requirement that he do so.

One paradigmatically modern example of "trouble getting started" is when one follows through with social rite without actually circumcising one's own heart. This seems exceedingly common, and this predicament is a barrier to Christian unity and communal strength.

On the other end, we see numerous issues related to the material distractions and comforts of modern life. Have you ever noticed how a sizeable number of pastors and impassioned Christian figures have either dealt with substance abuse or have lived through physical or sexual abuse? The easiest explanation is that *tough times tend to draw man towards sources of divine inspiration*. When one is down on one's knees pleading for help and mercy, it becomes natural to find someone *above them* to plead to. Contrarily, when one is flying high and feeling more powerful than his peers, it

---

3. Romans 2:25–29.

PART IV: Coming in from the Rain (But Away from the Spirit)

can become quite difficult to submit oneself to any higher authority. Does it seem likely that a multibillionaire with more shiny toys than 99.999 percent of his peers would willingly submit himself to a Master? In Matthew 10:23–25, Jesus says as much:

> [23] Jesus looked around and said to his disciples, "How hard it is for the rich to enter the Kingdom of God!" [24] This amazed them. But Jesus said again, "Dear children, it is very hard to enter the Kingdom of God. [25] In fact, it is easier for a camel to go through the eye of a needle than for a rich person to enter the Kingdom of God!"[4]

In the modern age, we face problems getting to God on two main fronts—problems of (i) legalistic, social ritual and problems of (ii) the distraction of material possessions.

GETTING SIDETRACKED

In Jesus's Parable of the Sower, we see the various ways man can become spiritually sidetracked.[5] We have the Blind Heart, the Rocky Heart, the Rebellious (Thorny) Heart and the Full Heart. There is no one kind of heart that is more endemic of the modern age than the others. The Blind Heart, the Rocky and the Rebellious are all common. The great spiritual pulls that are materiality and sensuality impact the believer's initial disposition (the Blind Heart), his staying power (the Rocky), and his overall commitment to Christ (the Thorny).

One type of heart closely related to the modern predicament of "spiritual ADHD" is the Blind Heart. When one does not apply sufficient focus to one's Savior and merely recites legalistic-sounding pledges or makeshift verses, there is no surprise when one's seed gets swiped up by the enemy. This is at once a theological problem and a social problem. Yet, the Blind Heart is not the only condition created by our modern afflictions. The Rocky Heart also thrives in today's age, with our worship of "efficiency" and "time-saving." The modern mind may be tempted to take the spiritually "quick and easy" route, giving one's heart as a one-time spiritual "buy-in." Unfortunately, heart-to-Heart communion with Jesus and the Lord is not the content of an infomercial. It is deep and heavy stuff.

---

4. ESV.
5. Matthew 13.

Spiritual Procrastination

Those who become deeply embedded in the modern lifestyle, with all of its sensuality and spiritual distractions, quickly grow a Rebellious Heart, lined with thick foliage and thorns. When one takes full refuge in the island of pleasure and procrastination, it becomes commonsensical to *partially* commit to the Lord. From a standpoint of self-interest and pleasure-seeking, why should I *fully* commit and submit to the Lord, if He will always be there to forgive whatever sensual and material missteps I make? It is in this sense that the Rebellious Heart is perhaps the most redolent of the modern condition. Additionally, there is often a lurking suspicion in the back of the modern mind: what if these brilliant scientists and physicists are right about the universe? What if we're all just floating around on a meaningless speck of dust? The modern man must take heed of James 1:6, "But he must ask [for wisdom] in faith, without doubting, because he who doubts is like a wave of the sea, blown and tossed by the wind."[6]

LAST-MINUTE PROPULSION

It is the Rebellious Heart we just discussed that facilitates such "last-minute propulsions." Let's take a look at something which sums up the modern issue of spiritual procrastination perfectly, a brief Q&A exchange on the website of Billy Graham's Evangelistic Association, *www.billygraham.org*. Here's the question:

> Q: My cousin has always lived kind of a wild life, but he says he isn't worried because he plans to turn to God just before he dies, and he says God will forgive him and let him into Heaven. Is this right?[7]

This, as I mentioned recently, is the rational choice for the modern man. When one is immersed in the world and all of its luxuries, it can be extremely difficult to lift one's eyes up towards the Lord. Alas, if we continue to spiritually procrastinate in this way, God won't be granting us any excuses. The great Billy Graham answers the question perfectly:

> A: The Bible says that God is willing to forgive anyone who turns to Him in repentance and faith, and sincerely puts their faith in Jesus Christ for their salvation—even at the last minute.

6. ESV.
7. Graham, "Can I Live a Wild Life?" para. 1.

PART IV: Coming in from the Rain (But Away from the Spirit)

> Your cousin, however, is unwise in thinking he can turn to God at the last minute and be saved; in fact, he is in grave spiritual danger. For one thing, we can't truly receive Christ without sincerely repenting of our sins. But *if he's unwilling to do that now, what reason does he have for thinking he'll be willing to do it later*? Jesus' first sermon included these words: "Repent and believe the good news!" (Mark 1:15). (emphasis added)[8]

The boldfaced portion is an absolutely crucial insight into the nature of the Rebellious Heart. There is a sort of "spiritual inertia" at work within the heart of man. The more he spiritually procrastinates, the less fertile his spiritual soil becomes. If someone's heart is hardened enough to feel little or no guilt in putting off repentance, there won't be some suddenly appearing "magic cure" in one's later years. Sooner or later, this person will have to make the choice to *reflect*. If this person perseveres in genuine and humble reflection, he will be well on his way to genuine repentance. Otherwise, he will have to hope for a genuine miracle.

A SENSE OF PARALYSIS AND FEELING OVERWHELMED

I touched a bit on spiritual paralysis earlier when I discussed the rigidness of modern theology. We saw the myriad verbal rituals that serve as formal "initiation" into the arms of Christ and how these rigidities can hinder positive spiritual development. No doubt, these formalities can make spiritual newcomers feel overwhelmed. But there is also much more to the topic of spiritual paralysis. Even after one has been spiritually born anew, one can face stumbling blocks of spiritual stress and pressure. I'll break up these issues into three main categories: (i) Am I Doing This Right?, (ii) Why Am I Doing This? and (iii) What More Can I Do?

Am I Doing This Right?

There are more than 200 distinct Christian denominations in the United States.[9] And throughout these 200 American denominations there are numerous different brands and flavors. On the *global* scale, there are 45,000 different Christian denominations, each one with its own unique

---

8. Graham, "Can I Live a Wild Life?" para. 1–3.
9. See Pew's "Global Christianity" report.

scriptural spin and rites of worship.[10] The National Association of Evangelicals has admitted that nearly 60 percent of evangelical leaders have changed denominations since childhood, and the Christian Science Monitor states that half of all Americans have changed their religious denomination at least once in their lives. And although there is significant correlation between membership of certain denominations and geographical location, there is much strife and overlap between the numerous Christian groups in America.

Let's consider what's at stake here.

As believers, we stand before a two-forked road. One fork is "Damnation St.," heading straight to Hell. The other fork is "Salvation Rd.," a straight shot to Heaven. Although there is a sizeable minority of believers who refuse to acknowledge the former fork's existence, the crushing reality of these two forks is something that rests heavily upon the average believer. Given the nature of the spiritual "gamble," it can be tempting for the modern believer to lapse into *hyper-analytical theism*. With so many theological options and such a high price to pay for "missing the mark," the modern believer can easily spin himself in spiritual circles. In fact, this is all coming from personal experience. I still struggle with escaping this mindset.

Why Am I Doing This?

Given the world of spiritual doubt and material temptation we find ourselves in, the modern believer can sometimes ask himself, "Why am I doing this?" One glances over at his non-believer friends, immersing themselves in the finest of worldly pleasures—from drugs and sex to unbridled ambition and material achievement—and begins to doubt one's life choice. It should go without saying that the believer of fertile spiritual soil should feel little unease of this sort. But those who have been thoroughly "materialized" in their outlook are in grave spiritual danger of succumbing to this malady.

This kind of spiritual envy is not the only cause of a "Why am I doing this?" crisis. Sometimes all it takes to engender spiritual doubt is to catch a less than savory gut-feeling about their fellow believers. This sort of angst is summed up perfectly by the book title, *I'm Fine with God . . . It's Christians I Can't Stand* (2008). The classic case of this hatred is derived from ostensible rampant hypocrisy and judging, self-righteous attitudes in the

---

10. See Pew's "Global Christianity" report.

church. Although we can be sure this kind of spiritual doubt existed even in ancient days, there is little doubt that it has been magnified by modern spiritual trend.

What More Can I Do?

The average modern church has become increasingly monetized and "beaucratizied." Within it exists a plethora of titles and functions, each with its own unique and privileged social status. Anytime such an institution exists, there is bound to be judgement, envy and drama. This is human nature.

The modern phenomenon of the "workaholic" has wriggled into the church with disastrous consequences. Once the modern believer finds himself embedded in such a competitive and bureaucratic atmosphere, the scourge that is works-based theology lurks around the corner. The measuring stick of righteousness is plucked from Heaven and eagerly and exactingly used *by man* to measure the righteousness of himself and his neighbor. This is a level above mere "self-righteousness." We can call this modern spiritual sickness "social-righteousness," and it is a grave malady indeed.

Where such "social-righteousness" abounds, the believer is trapped in a cycle of measuring and subsequently questioning one's works. Am I volunteering enough? Am I contributing enough? Am I connected enough? This is a never-ending spiritual battle, and it keeps the believer from bearing full spiritual fruit.

IMPAIRED SENSE OF TIME

It might not be obvious how this facet of inattention can fit into a religious mold. How can one have an impaired sense of time when it comes to the spiritual? One crucial way this fits with religion is in perceived length and perceived value of one's physical life. To someone deeply in love with this world and all of its comforts and pleasures, the value and length of physical life can be *overstated*. Much prosperity gospel theology relies upon the gross overstatement of our physical lives. To the adherents of this sort of theology, the material world is the ultimate stage, and it is our duty to "live it up," channeling power from the spiritual realm into our daily lives.

The modern church's obsession with social role and bureaucratic hierarchy also contributes to a lopsided sense of our time on this earth.

Spiritual Procrastination

Where contributions and deeds are scrupulously counted and measured, so are one's days, weeks and years. And if a year has gone by and we haven't received *visible* material and career-based benefits, then are we really "using our time wisely?"

Such warped emphasis on our physical lives contradicts scripture. There are myriad verses stressing the transience and mercuriality of man's material life. Two prominent examples are Psalm 78:39, "He remembered that they were but flesh, a passing breeze that does not return."[11] and Job 8:9, "For we were born only yesterday and know nothing, and our days on earth are but a shadow."[12]

FEAR OF FAILURE

As I mentioned in the "A Sense of Paralysis and Feeling Overwhelmed" subchapter, the wager of faith that is Christianity has extremely high stakes. It's literally (eternal) life or (eternal) death. The most obvious "fear of failure" in modern religion is intertwined with the nature of this bet. There is also the *social* version of fear of failure, and this variety is becoming especially pronounced in the modern day.

One of the most prominent "fear of failures" in today's church is that of social *underperformance*. Given that church is a fixture in the believer's social world, the expectation to signal righteousness to one's fellow believers is a powerful norm. For example, let's take a look at the potential consequences of such a norm:

"Hey Kathy! It's nice to see you here this week."
"Hey Rob! Nice to see you as well."
"So where's Steve? [her husband] . . . Doesn't he normally come with?"
"Oh . . . Yeah . . . Um he's not feeling too well today."
"Awh . . . I'm sorry to hear that."
***
Rob gets home to his wife
"Hey babe. Yeah, church went great. But you know Kathy. . . ? Her husband wasn't there, and something just seemed off. I'm thinking they split. I never pictured them as the type to ever consider divorce. . . "

I don't mean to condemn any believers with this. Chances are, we've all acted like this! But the root of this modern issue actually lies far deeper

---

11. ESV.
12. ESV.

than the individual believer and his behavior. The core issue is this—our modern style of worship does not foster neighborly love and connection, i.e., the man-to-man covenant that was so important in the ancient days. The average modern church is a one-stop shop. Going to church is now more similar to going to the grocery store than going to commune with fellow believers and the Almighty. Everything is out of whack.

Given this sort of social pressure that abounds in the modern church, today's believer can be excused for being wary of the religious social scene. This, of course, is part of the reason Christians sometimes get a bad rap. There is a sort of insidious, cutthroat sociality within today's churches, and it has begun to seep into theology at large in many instances.

CONCLUSION

Spiritual ADHD is not a cute little name for a made-up problem. What I've termed spiritual ADHD is an extremely serious issue that calls for much theological attention and deliberation. We must remember that it is up to us, as children of the Lord, to utilize the *free will* He so graciously endowed us with. We cannot expect this modern scourge to be graciously wiped away if we fail to do the requisite work on earth, in His will. I pray this can serve as a theological clarion call.

CHAPTER 18

SPIRITUAL MASTURBATION

"A cold, self-righteous prig who goes regularly to church may be far nearer to Hell than a prostitute."

—C.S. LEWIS[1]

THERE IS A CHANCE the title of this chapter may seem out of place or needlessly vulgar. Although the average believer is inundated with sexualized innuendo, he is still very wary to bring up sex, especially in conjunction with religion. The mere mention of such a taboo as "masturbation" is enough to turn the average believer into a faux prude. All this aside, sometimes a title is just a title, no dirty undertones or subliminal messages. This title is indeed *just a title*. The topic I have in mind is not even a sexual one; it's a *spiritual* one.

My goal in mentioning the infamous "M-word" is to draw a metaphor between it and a certain modern spiritual trend. There is a kind of modern theology that advocates spiritual behaviors similar to the physical act of the M-word. This theology—both a part of and beyond the "prosperity gospel" and the "little gods theology"—is at once extremely appealing and virulently dangerous.

---

1. Originally from Lewis's *Mere Christianity*. Taken from *The Complete C. S. Lewis*, 89.

PART IV: Coming in from the Rain (But Away from the Spirit)

Let's put all of our prudish and immature attitudes aside for a bit and think about what masturbation is. Masturbation is an act of *personal* stimulation, by oneself and for oneself. It is the ultimate form of *selfish* gratification. Putting aside the question of whether or not physical masturbation is explicitly mentioned in the Word, I will focus on the *spiritual* connotations that it affords us.

Back in Chapter IV, "God's Man," we saw Samuel 18:3 and the covenant of friendship between and Jonathan and David. It is said that Jonathan initiated this covenant with David because he "loved him as himself." This is the perfect example of something diametrically *opposite* of masturbation. The covenant of friendship in Samuel 18:3 was a *selfless* act, infused with sacrifice and submission. This selfless man-to-man covenant is what the modern church desperately needs to bring into its walls. We live in a world in which the "invisible hand" that is self-interest and self-achievement has propelled believers so far apart that such a covenant is nearly unfathomable.

Let's take a look at a prime example of spiritual masturbation in action. These words come from the wife of a widely popular megachurch pastor:

> So I just want to encourage every one of us to realize... When we obey God, we're not doing it for God. I mean, that's one way to look at it. We're doing it for ourselves. Because God takes pleasure when we're happy. That's the thing that gives him the greatest joy this morning. So I want you to know this morning, just do good for your own self; do good because God wants you to be happy. When you come to church, *when you worship him, you're not doing it for God*, really. *You're doing it for yourself.* Because that's what makes God happy! (emphasis added)[2]

This is New Age self-help wrapped in a religious package. There's no getting out of that. At the bottom layer, this sort of theology advocates moral relativism. It makes no room for spiritual or moral absolutes, and it is completely self-serving.

There is a Christian blog called Fourth Year Ministries which published an article called "Self-Centered Theology" back in 2015. This article also gives us a perfect summation of the theology of so-called spiritual masturbation:

> This false gospel appeals to the desires and felt-needs of the individual.
> This false gospel elevates the person above what is appropriate.

2. I won't share her name here, but I will cite the source in the back.

Spiritual Masturbation

This false gospel fails to mention or emphasize biblical repentance. A gospel without repentance is no gospel at all.[3]

In reading these, one cannot help but be pulled back to ponder on the *prosperity gospel* and its roots. On the face of it, the prosperity gospel checks two of the three above boxes. The prosperity gospel appeals to man's desire for wealth and power, and it elevates man to "little god" status. Of course, the analysis of an entire theology is not so simple as making such sweeping declarations. We must again consider the nature and sources of the prosperity gospel's leanings.

In Chapter V, "God's Theatre," we saw a trend of theology called "New Thought." This style of thought was all but founded by the American mentalist and "mesmerist" Phineas Quimby.[4] Mesmerism is an outdated term for *hypnotism*, and it is quite clear that Quimby had little to no regard for the written Word of God. He was something of a syncretist who liked to fuse ancient philosophy with modern method and science. Alas, Quimby's writings went on to ignite a full-fledged spiritual movement in America.

If one makes the journey to *www.newthought.info/beliefs/nt_beliefs.htm* one will find a slew of interesting and bizarre statements. Under the "New Thought Today" banner the group lists seventeen "Principles of the New Millennium." The two most relevant of these statements for our purposes are the following :

11. We affirm that we are spiritual beings having a physical experience and as we come into alignment with the laws of the universe, we harmonize with That That [sic] is and can thus heal, prosper, and live in balance and peace.

12. We affirm that our mental states influence our interpretation of our experiences and that through the principle of co-creation / partnership our thoughts can be carried forward into manifestation and become our experience in daily living.[5]

Besides the palpably cult-like connotation of these statements, we can glean two pieces of crucial insight from them. We see the claim that if "we harmonize with [God]," then we can "heal, prosper, and live in balance and

---

3. "Self-Centered Theology," para. 11–13.
4. Bowler, *Blessed* (Oxford), 13–14.
5. "New Millennium," para. 10–11.

peace." We also see the assertion that "our thoughts can be carried forward into manifestation and become our experience in daily living."

When think about all this a bit deeper, things get really bizarre. Taken at face value, these two claims aren't that shocking or offensive to the average modern person. These two statements are more or less implicitly accepted. The modern man is so obsessed with himself that he can hardly fathom a world in which he is anything other than powerful and spiritually beautiful.

The issue with these statements is their *improper emphasis*. Statement 11 takes man's spirituality and ability to "align with the universe" and "heal, prosper, and live in balance and peace" as a given. Statement 12 posits that man alone can alter the physical world, through his own thought and optimism.

We must remember that *nothing* is possible without our Lord. Without Him we hold no authority whatsoever.

Let's briefly return to Kate Bowler' eclectic *Blessed: A History of the American Prosperity Gospel* (2018):

> African American Pentecostalism resonated with metaphysical religion, a connection that proved to be electric. Pentecostalism provided a familiar narrative of sin, repentance, and salvation, sealed with Jesus' death and resurrection. New Thought, in contrast, persisted as a religion of utility. In other words, people found in it a religion they could use. The resulting messages combined a Christological framework with the mechanism of mental magic, guaranteeing believers the ability to change their circumstances by tapping into new spiritual powers.[6]

Of course, the prosperity gospel is not a solely African American trend. It is not confined to one denomination or locale. To get an idea of what the overarching framework of the prosperity gospel looks like (and, by implication, the gospel of "spiritual masturbation") we can look at the writings and teachings of Norman Vincent Peale.

In the 1930s, with great scientific advancement and a burgeoning "counter culture," psychology collided with theology, resulting in what was called "pastoral psychology." Books such as *The Art of Ministering* (1936) and *The Art of Counseling* (1939) sought to bring modern methods of psychology and attention to bear upon the teaching of scripture. Some preachers of the thirties took advantage of this zeitgeist. Norman Vincent

---

6. Bowler, *Blessed* (PhD thesis version), 50.

Peale was one these preachers, enlisting a professor of psychiatry at Cornell University Medical School to help counsel his parishioners. Several years later, Peal and this professor went on to co-author a book called *Faith is the Answer: A Psychiatrist and Pastor Discuss Your Problems* (1940).[7]

None of the above rings any major alarm bells. Not quite yet! Although the history behind this theology seems rather mundane, it is no understatement to say that this fusion of psychiatry and theology opened the door to a slew of theological ailments, plaguing the church for decades. Which "ailments" am I speaking of? First and foremost—the improper spiritual elevation of man. All other modern theological illnesses have spawned from this tainted seed.

In 1952, Peale published *The Power of Positive Thinking*. Drawing from Bowler's assessment of this work in her *Blessed* (2018), we see that this work offered the bold statement that "God's power could be harnessed by a spirit and method by which we can control and even determine life's circumstances."[8] Bowler then adds that "Peale taught that any person could access God's power through positive thinking, which directed spiritual energy toward the attainment of health, self-esteem, or business acumen."[9] Bowler ends this discussion with the telling assertion that "[Peale] invoked Jesus as *Teacher, not Savior* . . . "[10] (emphasis added)

Where we turn Christ into Teacher, we invert the natural subordination of man to God. The entire point of having as glorious of a Savior as Christ Jesus is that in submitting to Him, we begin to break off tidbits of his heavenly wisdom. The entire dichotomy of Christ as Teacher versus Christ as Savior is an invalid one. Christ cannot be Teacher without being Savior, and He cannot be Savior without being Teacher. The problem is that the more emphasis we put upon the Teaching side, the more worldly and self-concerned we humans will become. If we get carried away with Christ the teacher, we will forget that it is not *our* will that matters here on earth. We must constantly remind ourselves that it is the Will that reigns supreme on earth, as it does in Heaven.

The modern world is obsessed with *results* and *success*. These are the core principles of today. Moreover, we have been inculcated with advertising in all of its nefarious forms. In order for us to achieve personal "results"

---

7. See Bowler, *Blessed* (Oxford), 55–57.
8. Bowler, *Blessed* (Oxford), 57.
9. Bowler, *Blessed* (Oxford), 57.
10. Bowler, *Blessed* (Oxford), 57.

and "success" we must advertise ourselves. This is the essence of the resume. Online dating apps have forced many of us to advertise our romantically appealing qualities, and our culture of superficial politeness forces us to advertise our happiness and virtue to one another. It is little wonder that spiritual masturbation has gotten such a stronghold! As we saw with Norman Vincent Peale and his *The Power of Positive Thinking*, there is an allure to thinking that us humans can *demand* what we want from the "universe." There is a sexiness in believing that the physical world is a *plaything* of man.

Although the times have changed and the milieu is startlingly different, the wisdom of Luke 9:23–25 still stands as an example for us to heed.

> 23 Then he said to them all: "Whoever wants to be my disciple must deny themselves and take up their cross daily and follow me. 24 For whoever wants to save their life will lose it, but whoever loses their life for me will save it. 25 What good is it for someone to gain the whole world, and yet lose or forfeit their very self?
> 26 Whoever is ashamed of me and my words, the Son of Man will be ashamed of them when he comes in his glory and in the glory of the Father and of the holy angels.

Us moderns must learn the wisdom of *denying ourselves*. The more we continue to bury our spiritual heads in the sand, procrastinating and indulging in the material fruits of the modern world, the longer this world will be divorced from God's Will. Spiritual masturbation and procrastination must end.

CHAPTER 19

Don't Forget to Worship Your Pastor (and Your Denomination Too!)

"If God created us in his own image, we have more than reciprocated."
—Voltaire

"One must love God first, and only then can one love one's closest of kin and neighbors. We must not be idols to one another, for such is not the will of God."
—Elder Thaddeus of Vitovnica

The modern man might blissfully assume that the worship of and undue submission to God's "earthly representatives" (AKA the clergy) halted with Luther's ninety-five theses in 1517. Alas, although today's Christians do not desperately empty their pockets to purchase indulgences from their pastors, many do succumb to just as spiritually grave a predicament.

It is one thing to admire and respect your pastor. It is another thing entirely to *worship* him.

Let's consider what exactly I mean by "worship," because this is a tricky term to deal with. Let this much be clear—one need not fall to his feet or cower in obsequiousness in front of his pastor to worship him. This

PART IV: Coming in from the Rain (But Away from the Spirit)

point centers on the nature of an *idol*, a notion that is front and center in the Word.

It is easy for one to fall into the trap of thinking an idol has to be *physical*. But the more we probe the Word the more we realize that this needn't be the case. There are three key verses that indicate to us that idolatry is beyond mere physicality—Exodus 20:3, "You shall have no other gods before me."; Colossians 2:8, "See to it that no one takes you captive by philosophy and empty deceit, according to human tradition, according to the elemental spirits of the world, and not according to Christ."[1] ; and Luke 12:34, "For where your treasure is, there will your heart be also."[2] Each one of these verses leaves open the option for more abstract, intangible forms of idolatry.

One needn't treat his pastor like the Queen of England, groveling over him and catering to him, to have him become his personal idol. When a believer simply takes the words of his pastor above or on equal footing with the Word of the Lord, he is committing idolatry. It is an unfortunate fact that the modern believer is able to tuck himself away in a spiritual corner, believing that since he isn't a member of a zany cult, he doesn't worship his pastor. The idol that is religious authority is an extremely insidious one; to detect it is to meditate and thoroughly reflect upon one's own spiritual inclinations.

Once one's pastor becomes his idol, his heart can become dangerously close to being severed from the unadulterated Word. Where one places more faith in an authority figure's scriptural interpretation than in his own spiritual intuition of the Lord's Word, spiritual danger is afoot. It is for these reasons crucial that the modern realize the great liberty of scriptural interpretation that is seen in pastors far and wide.

I mentioned several chapters ago the great number of Christian denominations—there are over 200 distinct denominations in America alone. What I didn't yet mention is the great conviction that many of these denominations have in their own "brand" of worship and scriptural interpretation. A perfect example of this denominational advertising can be prominently found in the issue of tongues or *glossolalia*.

Two of the most eloquent voices on the matter—John MacArthur and Michael Brown—have two diametrically opposed views on the subject. Both gentlemen claim to draw their positions from scripture alone. In 2013

1. ESV.
2. ESV.

Don't Forget to Worship Your Pastor

MacArthur published his *Strange Fire: The Danger of Offending the Holy Spirit with Counterfeit Worship*, which attacks much of the Pentecostal, Charismatic body of theology, most prominently the practice of *glossolalia*. Just two years later, Brown cranked out a retort, with his *Authentic Fire: A Response to John MacArthur's Strange Fire*. This dialectical dance of MacArthur and Brown is unsettling. How can two men of Christ leave the Book with such mutually conflicting views of its content?

Unfortunately, I can't even begin to address the bulk of such a deep question. What I can do is stress the importance of forging a strong *personal* and *communal* relationship with Christ.

The interpretation of scripture has always been a tricky and contentious business, but once scriptural interpretation gets rapidly packaged, branded and sold to eager "customers," there is much theological danger afoot. That is, once the materialism of the modern world takes hold *in the church*, strange things begin to happen.

This phenomenon of modern "interpretational marketing" can best be described as "religious production," much like factory or assembly line production. Many modern theologians take to interpretation with such ferocity and ambition that they become cunning businessmen, more eager for the "brand" than the Spirit. This manner of theological production places a massively undue emphasis upon man and his capacities of *structure building*. Although "structure building" might initially sound rather esoteric or abstract, it has a perfect scriptural metaphor in the tower of Babel. It is a sad likelihood that the average modern believer sees little problem in the eager construction of such worldly structures. This is likely because they don't quite grasp what the construction at Babel *means*.

The Christly counter to the tower of Babel appears in 1 Peter 2, where we see the believer described as like a "living stone" which is used to build a "spiritual house," a "holy priesthood." Then we see Christ himself described as the "chief cornerstone" in Ephesians 2:20. In these verses we glimpse an alternative to the worldly, man-centered construction undertaken in Babel. In these verses we see that all *earthly* construction is unstable if it fails to place Christ as its cornerstone and recognize the *homogeneity* of the "living stones." This "spiritual house" which will serve as a holy priesthood is one, unified construction. There is no "spiritual house of the Pentecostals" or "spiritual house of the Catholics." There is One spiritual house in Christ.

Having established this viewpoint—this alternative to Babel-esque, worldly construction—I'd like to work towards explaining the danger of

PART IV: Coming in from the Rain (But Away from the Spirit)

buying into any one man's "brand" of scriptural interpretation. In reference to 1 Peter 2, I think it is perfectly acceptable to wonder "If Christ is the cornerstone then who is the architect, and who is the builder?" And I think it's just as acceptable to answer, "*God* is the architect, and the *Holy Spirit* is the builder." This is our answer to how we must organize ourselves on this earth: we are all as living stones, inhabiting the spiritual house whose cornerstone is Christ Jesus, whose builder is the Spirit and whose architect and visionary is the Lord Almighty. There is no room in this construction for mini, knockoff spiritual houses. There is no room for unilateral dominion of man.

The trouble with today's interpretational climate—in which myriad pastors stake their claims upon the "proper" reading of the Word—is that there is a knockoff spiritual house corresponding to each one of these "definitive" interpretations. The debate between John MacArthur and Michael Brown is a microcosm that resembles today's theological predicament at large. Currently, there is a spiritual house comprising the MacArthur adherents, and there is a spiritual house composed of Brown adherents. These houses stand apart, because no house inherits sufficient structural integrity from a contradictory, mutually misshapen foundation. Thankfully, *both* brands of interpretation at least incorporate Christ Jesus as their cornerstone. This alone ensures that there is still hope for structural integration between these houses.

The antidote to this modern sectarianism is a fundamental shift in how believers interact and worship. In Chapter V, "God's Theatre," we saw the stark contrast between modern -day theological organization and ancient *communal* interaction. It is a sad fact that today communalism (*no, not communism*) and its guiding principles are unfairly lumped into the wastebin of "radical" ideas. When one searches the term "communalism" and arrives at its Wikipedia page, one receives the dry sounding, textbook definition: "Communalism is a political philosophy and economic system that integrates communal ownership and confederations of highly localized independent communities."[3] This definition is so far removed from the spiritual and social roots of the idea that it hardly deserves consideration.

What I mean by communalism meshes strongly with κοινωνία (*koinonia*) the Greek word for fellowship or communion. In the New Testament, the word *koinonia* is applied to astoundingly diverse contexts, from the

---

3. https://en.wikipedia.org/wiki/Communalism.

blood and the body of Christ to the common nature of mankind; *koinonia* is a wonderfully versatile word and concept.

Now is a great time to reintroduce a verse I showed in Chapter V. This verse, Ephesians 4:1–6, highlights our pressing need of spiritual, denominational, and theological unification into one body in Christ:

> **Unity and Maturity in the Body of Christ**
>
> **4** As a prisoner for the Lord, then, I urge you to live a life worthy of the calling you have received. **2** Be completely humble and gentle; be patient, bearing with one another in love. **3** Make every effort to keep the unity of the Spirit through the bond of peace. **4** There is one body and one Spirit, just as you were called to one hope when you were called; **5** one Lord, one faith, one baptism; **6** one God and Father of all, who is over all and through all and in all.

In this light, things may seem blindingly simple. "Why don't we just double down on our ecumenism and unite all denominations into one?" Such a longing—though it is certainly an admirable one—is rather naïve. We are at a point where the various denominations have diverged so sharply from one another that such unification will be no easy feat. Oftentimes today's ecumenism falls victim to the same theological ills that plague the modern church at large. That very same habit of man-fueled *structure building* I mentioned earlier often carries over into the fight to unify the Christian faith. According to this "structure building" perspective, we must obsolete all denominations in order to usher in "The denomination," the ultimate set of theological rules.

If we follow the wisdom in 1 Peter 2 and Ephesians 2:20, we realize that the only "ultimate" denomination we need is the Blood of Christ and the fellowship therewithin. We mustn't seek a human fix for this.

PART V

Getting off the Couch and into the Spiritual House

CHAPTER 20

THE FORKED PATH

"For you will certainly carry out God's purpose, however you act, but it makes a difference to you whether you serve like Judas or like John."

—C.S. Lewis[1]

It is a bit cliché to point out that we have only two options. This is a technique that is used all too much, even in instances where there are far more than two choices. In this case, however, there can be no doubt that we do have *only* two options. Each of these is directly opposed to one another.

On one hand, we can continue to bolster the individual man, his selfish desires and earthly lusts, making sure theological emphasis is directed that way. On the other, we can ensure that the individual man is humbled and situated beneath the Almighty, while still acknowledging his privileged place in God's Kingdom.

Throughout this book I've spoken about the balance between submission and desire. In Chapter VIII, "No Spiritual Luxury Without *Spiritual Submission*" I gave a distinction between craving and desire. The former draws man away from the Lord and towards his selfish desires, while the latter can bring him closer to God. In modernity, where the lines between comfort and pain have been boldfaced, we tend to view the submission versus desire dichotomy as a mutually exclusive one. We tend to think if we

---

1. Lewis, *The Problem of Pain*, 99.

PART V: Getting off the Couch and into the Spiritual House

are to properly submit, we must expunge ourselves of all desire. This is in fact far from the case.

In such theological skirmishes as that between John MacArthur and Michael Brown we see the essential tension between *submission* and *spiritual communion*.[2] The former pastor finds it more important to emphasize submission, across all theological and personal domains. The latter gentleman thinks we should focus on our relationship with and the utilization of the Spirit. Both of these gentlemen believe that their views are buttressed solely by scripture and are, in some sense, *authoritative*. Although both pastors make excellent points, we cannot lose ourselves in this debate. In order to fully submit, I think we must keep our eyes on the spiritual house in Christ Jesus.

Although I stressed the great wisdom and sensibility of the ancient man, I do not intend to promote some sort of staid or morose theology of inert reverence. This is the exact opposite of what I wish to do. The attributes of the ancient man we should wish to replicate in the modern man are those of *desire-filled reverence* and deep and profound *recognition* of the Lord.

The ancient had an *acknowledgement* of the Spirit that imbued his soul, strengthening his connection with his brothers and sisters in Christ. It is these valuable, long-lost traits we should wish to reunite with man. It is this reverence and genuine desire for the Lord that can mollify one's soul and pave the path towards a selfless and integrated Christian community.

Moving on from this ideal picture of the world, let's discuss something a bit more pragmatic. Let's talk about the modern world and its reaction to such sentiments as "unification in Christ" and "collectivism." Why has modernity struggled so woefully with these two things?

Post-World War II modernity is an era highly skeptical of collectivism and all of its connotations. Alas, today collectivism is associated with such demons as Communism, Socialism and Anarchism, so much so that it has become taboo to discuss its merits, even in Christian contexts. Even from a raw, philosophical standpoint, the modern West has disparaged collectivism, starting most prominently with Karl Popper's tome *The Open Society and Its Enemies* (1945).

---

2. I refer here to MacArthur's book, *Strange Fire*, and to Brown's response, *Authentic Fire*. This debate centers on how believers are permitted to "use" the Holy Spirit. Are we permitted to channel the Spirit, or should we seek not to use it, as we are not worthy?

The Forked Path

Popper took it upon himself to trace the intellectual origins of totalitarianism, beginning with Plato and Aristotle and culminating in Hegel and Marx. Although Popper's book serves as a fine defense of capitalistic democracy against forces of centrally planned utopian schemes, it heaps undue blame on collectivism. Popper omits it from consideration. In tracing the evolution of political society, Popper distinguishes between the "closed society" and the "open society," lumping all varieties of collectivism into the former category. To him, only individualism and self-reliance can result in a truly free and democratic society, an "open" society. Below we see Popper discuss the changes that lead to an open society:

> [A]n open society may become, by degrees, what I should like to term an 'abstract society'. It may, to a considerable extent, lose the character of a concrete or real group of men, or of a system of such real groups. [. . .] We could conceive of a society in which men practically never meet face to face—in which all business is conducted by individuals in isolation who communicate by typed letters or by telegrams, and who go about in closed motor-cars. (Artificial insemination would allow even propagation without a personal element.) Such a fictitious society might be called a 'completely abstract or depersonalized society'.[3]

Popper never explicitly advocates for such a "completely abstract or depersonalized society," but he does leave it as a possibility. Despite his valiant defense against the evils of communism and totalitarianism, Popper is willing to accept a society in which men are utterly divorced from one another. He is willing to idolize a society where man-to-man covenant and communion are things of the distant past. With the ongoing "COVID-19" fiasco and ubiquitous "lockdowns," such a society is no longer a wild thought experiment; it is a looming reality. With the proliferation of serotonin-stimulating gadgets and apps, it has become vastly easier to tune out the world and its people completely.

We now have a pretty good idea of what this "forked path" is. On one side we have the "abstract society" which inevitably begets a dull and depersonalized "abstract theology," and on the other we have a society which fosters the Biblical values of fellowship, covenant and communion. The longer our theologies stay maniacally fixated on the individual and his powers, the more precariously we will teeter on the edge of a full-blown abstract society, brimming with abstract and depersonalized theology. The

---

3. Popper, *The Open Society*, 190–91.

PART V: Getting off the Couch and into the Spiritual House

closer we get to that edge, the further away we are from the spiritual house, the holy priesthood of believers *in* Christ, *for* Christ and *by* Christ.

CHAPTER 21

WHAT CAN BE DONE?

"At the heart of Galatians 2 is not an abstract individualized salvation, but a common meal. Paul does not want the Galatians to wait until they have agreed on all doctrinal arguments before they can sit down and eat together. Not to eat together is already to get the answer wrong. The whole point of his argument is that all those who belong to Christ belong at the same table with one another."
—N.T. Wright[1]

It is no easy endeavor to diagnose the ills of an era's worth of theology. One must be ever vigilant lest his own theological hubris mar the core goal—genuine unification under Christ.

I do not wish to present any sort of "ultimate," unifying theological "framework"; I do not wish to succumb to the "system building" approach that modern theology has been so thoroughly marinated in. I think the best possible strategy we can adopt is a pragmatic, cautious one. We must keep with the general notion that no one man (barring Christ) can ever hope to attain a flawless and unadulterated interpretation of scripture. We must become *spiritual foragers*, grazing on whatever bears Christly fruit.

Taking this route of what can best be called "theological pragmatism," we can draw inspiration from the late philosopher and psychologist

---

1. Wright, *For All God's Worth*, 109.

PART V: Getting off the Couch and into the Spiritual House

William James, founder of the philosophical movement known as "American Pragmatism."

The essence of our approach is distilled in this quote from James: "Pragmatism has to postpone dogmatic answer, for we do not yet know certainly which type of religion is going to work best in the long run."[2] Although James was never an explicit advocate of Christianity, we can fashion this maxim of philosophical pragmatism into a theological one: theological pragmatism must postpone the dogmatic answer, for man alone can never surely know which type of theology is *The* theology. As tempting as it may be to aggressively claim ultimate scriptural truth, such an approach is detrimental to the body of the church and the fellowship that binds it together.

I've already brought forth an initial "diagnosis," several times throughout this book. In Chapter XI, "The Introduction of Cushion" I offered a rough sketch of the worst portions of modern theology, terming it the *theology of cushion* or TOC:

> TOC: Although the Lord is our creator and sustainer, his role here on earth is to facilitate us and help us in our day-to-day, worldly actions and endeavors. The Lord has his domain—Heaven. And we have our domain—the earth. Although God does have some degree of control over our earth, our cultures and societies upon this earth ultimately shape who we are and how we come to God. There is no reason to make great sacrifices for the Lord or undergo great acts of personal submission, simply because we live in the modern day, and we have moved beyond that sort of thing. Our job on earth is to achieve successes for ourselves, but also to keep God in mind as we achieve.

Not every church or denomination falls victim to all of these ills. But many of these components pervade the modern theological landscape, and they are often difficult to recognize. In Chapter XI, after I gave the theology of cushion, I offered a rough "solution":

> First and foremost, we must strike a proper balance between (i) *individualism* and *collectivism* and (ii) *soul*, *spirit* and *Spirit*. After straightening out the above issues, we must find the middle ground between two extremes. On one end there is the prosperity gospel-like emphasis on the physical and on the other a Gnostic-like disdain for the physical realm. We must simultaneously find a way to restore the ancient emphasis on the community and on

---

2. James, *Pragmatism and Other Writings*, 131.

the Divine covenant. We must humble the modern man, without diminishing his connection to the Almighty.

I've mentioned that my distinction between soul and spirit is a pragmatic one; it does not reflect any adherence to denominational theology. What I mean by "soul" can best be summed up as the faculties of man in use when he is not directly communing with God or worshipping Him. These are man's "everyday" operations of mind, from his earthly intellect to his earthly emotions. What I mean by "spirit" is whatever faculties are used when man *is* communing with God or worshipping Him. Regardless of denominational overtones, I think this is a very helpful distinction to make.

The task of offering a potential "solution" to the state of modern theology and society is a topic worthy of a book in its own right (a far bigger book than this one!) Although I cannot hope to provide anything resembling a genuine solution, I will touch on some of the most important topics. I will focus on the relationship between (i) and (ii) above, splitting the discussion up into five main subchapters, (1) Individualism & Collectivism, (2) Individualism & Soul, (3) Individualism & Spirit, (4) Collectivism & Soul and (5) Collectivism & Spirit.

INDIVIDUALISM & COLLECTIVISM

The Oxford English Dictionary defines individualism as "the habit or principle of being independent and self-reliant." Individualism from this standpoint is not an intrinsically bad thing to possess. In terms of social and occupational life, every person needs some degree of independence and self-reliance. Yet, we must notice an extremely important distinction. There are *two* senses in which we can speak of individualism and collectivism.

We can talk about the pair in the personal sense or the societal sense.

When I said that individualism isn't a bad thing to possess, I was speaking in the *personal* sense. I was speaking in terms of what is beneficial for any given man, on his own. The sense in which the philosopher Karl Popper (mentioned above) spoke of individualism is the *societal* sense.[3] Popper thought it rational that the *interactions* between men be fundamentally individualistic. There is a huge difference between these two usages of the term individualism.

---

3. Popper, *The Open Society*.

PART V: Getting off the Couch and into the Spiritual House

The popular Christian magazine, *The Banner*, has a wonderfully apt article called "The Heresy of Individualism." The article opens with a poignant and extremely relevant point:

> Researchers have studied veterans from the war in Afghanistan who have had trouble readjusting upon returning home. Many face depression, substance abuse, or even thoughts of suicide. Often, when questioned, they express a desire to return to the war. But that's not because they were fervent believers in war's purpose. Instead, they missed deeply their belonging to their platoon.[4]

This shows that even from a *personal* standpoint, too much individualism can be harmful. This fact also highlights modern society's lack of cohesive and collective networks of social support.

The article then goes on to mention the same point I've struggled to make throughout this book—God's ideal arrangement of men is a *collective*, communal one.

> Biblical wisdom has a different starting point. God's saving work always moves toward creating a faithful community of God's people. The inspiring stories of the Old Testament are framed around calling, liberating, and leading the people of Israel as a covenant community. The fulcrum of God's justice always falls on the side of shaping the shared life of a people whose hospitality and faithfulness reflect the covenantal love of God. It's not about me; it's about the "we."[5]

This much is scripturally airtight; this is the Will on earth. But just because we have a clear Biblical directive, this does not mean we are in for an easy journey. It is an extremely tricky task to strike the proper balance between individualism and collectivism on the *societal* level.

We must steer clear of grand, utopian schemes of organization, keeping in mind the great atrocities caused by regimes *claiming* to work in the interest of the collective. We must resist placing undue emphasis on the organization of society and economy, neglecting the role of the individual man and his spiritual growth and transformation. I think that the history of society is largely the history of the *overstatement* of man's external conditions, at the expense of his inner life and progression.

---

4. Granberg-Michaelson, "The Heresy of Individualism," para. 1.
5. Granberg-Michaelson, "The Heresy of Individualism," para. 7.

What Can Be Done?

We can get a better grasp on the proper balance between individualism and collectivism by re-examining the verses of 1 Peter 2, the discussion of a "spiritual house." These verses state that the believer is like a "living stone," a crucial component in the construction of a communal society in Christ.

If we stick with the metaphor of building and construction we can ask, "What is it that *separates* man (building stones) from one another?" and "What is it that *unites* man (building stones) with one another?" But before we dive into the answers to these questions, let's remember what we saw in relation to the role of the Lord and the Spirit. I offered this—*God* is the architect, and the *Holy Spirit* is the builder. Making things extremely simple, this means that the adhesive between the stones is *chosen* by God and is *applied* by the Holy Spirit.

Let's take a bit closer look at the "adhesive" and the "stones" in the spiritual house. We must recognize that the adhesive is everywhere the same substance. No matter the stone, the adhesive around it is the same. Given this, if there is any collectivism to be had, it will necessarily incorporate this property. It is also the case that all of the *stones* are of the *same substance*. Each one of us possess an immaterial soul, and we were all fashioned by the Lord. In terms of Christ Jesus, we see that although He is made of the substance of mere men (He is a stone as well), it is His privileged position (the corner stone) in the spiritual house that gives Him His identity and power. On top of this, we must not forget that every stone (child of God) has his/her own unique position in the spiritual house in Christ.

The metaphor of the spiritual house also reminds us of the proper role of individualism in a Christly society. The *only* individualism to be had lies in the various God-given positions or *roles* of His children. It is counter to Scripture to seek individualism anywhere else. We cannot hubristically assume that we ourselves are made of some special or privileged substance, and we certainly cannot assume that our adhesive is somehow stronger or more unique than any other's. Just as well, we cannot delude ourselves into thinking we're larger than the other stones. We cannot attempt to wriggle our way out of our God-given position, away from our neighboring stones and mortar. Doing so would not only ensure our departure from the spiritual house but compromise the foundation as a whole. The cooperation of every person is crucial.

With this metaphor we can clearly see how Christly collectivism differs from misshapen, earthly collectivism. The latter is inevitably based

PART V: Getting off the Couch and into the Spiritual House

on progression towards some ideal material and mental state, some sort of earthly utopia. The issue is that, without the knowledge of the spiritual house, its foundation and composition, there is no surefire way to know how to value the *individual* next to the *collective*. Under a utilitarian ethic, where maximal "happiness" for all humanity is sought after, wicked decisions are made in the name of "progress" towards the material "ideal." In such an ethic, there are no absolute guidelines under which the conduct of each individual can be placed. Immanuel Kant's deontological ethic, on the other hand, crumbles because although it is built upon rules as opposed to utility, it offers no means of finding or attaining these rules.[6] Christly collectivism proves itself to be above and beyond any fanciful intellectual construction of man, and the only "utility" it heeds is that of the Will of the Almighty.

INDIVIDUALISM & SOUL

Although it is easy to relegate the contributions of the rational mind and emotions to the spiritual dustbin, the soul plays an integral role in ensuring the spiritual house is sturdy. In the previous subchapter, I mentioned that individualism has both a *personal* sense and a *societal* sense. Given the spiritual house metaphor, we can already nullify *societal* individualism. However, individualism in the *personal* sense remains a highly powerful and influential spiritual factor. Perhaps the greatest sense in which personal individualism is useful is in the matter of scriptural discernment and independence. Let's take a look at something we saw back in Chapter XVIII, "Don't Forget to Worship Your Pastor (and Your Denomination Too!)":

> Once one's pastor becomes his idol, his heart can become dangerously close to being severed from the unadulterated Word. Where one places more faith in an authority figure's scriptural interpretation than in his own spiritual intuition of the Lord's Word, spiritual danger is afoot. It is for these reasons crucial that the modern realize the great liberty of scriptural interpretation that is seen in pastors far and wide.

Shortly after this, I mentioned the following:

---

6. Kant, *Groundwork of the Metaphysic of Morals*.

What Can Be Done?

This phenomenon of modern "interpretational marketing" can best be described as "religious production," much like factory or assembly line production. Many modern theologians take to interpretation with such ferocity and ambition that they become cunning businessmen, more eager for the "brand" than the Spirit. This manner of theological production places a massively undue emphasis upon man and his capacities of *structure building*. Although "structure building" might initially sound rather esoteric or abstract, it has a perfect scriptural metaphor in the tower of Babel.

It is this cocktail of (1) liberal interpretation of scripture and (2) the tendency toward structure building that necessitates a high level of personal individualism in the modern believer. If one is not an independent interpreter—adopting the art of scriptural "foraging"—one will be woefully susceptible to this pernicious modern influence. We must realize that the sort of personal individualism in Christ is vastly different than the kind modern secular society prescribes. In Chapter XIV, "Jesus the Life Coach," we saw an excerpt from a self-help book, *You Are a Badass: How to Stop Doubting Your Greatness and Start Living an Awesome Life*. Much of this tidbit showed us exactly how self-centered the philosophy of self-help is:

> *I* was so broke and clueless and sick of being such a weenie about really going for it in *my* life, that *I* was open for suggestions . . . Then *I* noticed how much better it made *me* feel . . . Then *I* became obsessed with it. Then *I* started loving it. . . . Wherever you happen to stand on the God issue, let me just say that that this whole improving your life thing is going to be a lot easier if you have an open mind about it. *Call it whatever you want—* God, Goddess, The Big Guy, The Universe, Source Energy, Higher Power, The Grand Poobah, gut, intuition, Spirit, The Force, The Zone, The Lord, The Vortex, The Mother Lode—*it doesn't matter.* (emphasis added)[7]

To the self-help-infused modern, personal individualism means— above all else—loving oneself. If there is religion or spirituality introduced, it ends up wrapping back in on the self. It is used as a tool of ego massage and self-adornment. All of this directly contradicts the wisdom provided in 1 Peter 2 and Ephesians 2:20 in which the spiritual house and the "cornerstone" of Christ are described.

---

7. Sincero, *You Are a Badass*, 29.

PART V: Getting off the Couch and into the Spiritual House

Before moving on, I will point out an additional property of the "living stones" in the spiritual house. Just as physical stones possess distinctive edges and surfaces, the living stones in Christ possess distinctive qualities of the soul. Some children of the Lord are naturally tough and assertive, others are more tender and sensitive. Some of us are more social and talkative and some of us are more introverted and reserved. Some are more intellectual and comfortable with ideas and logic, and some of us are more hands-on and physical workers and learners. The list goes on *ad infinitum*. Despite all of our differences, we have some pretty impressive commonalities—each and every one of us can work on our discernment and scriptural wisdom. We can all work on building the parts of our souls that foster a healthy personal individualism in Christ. This sort of personal improvement is the *real* "self-help."

INDIVIDUALISM & SPIRIT

A few paragraphs ago I mentioned the importance of cultivating discernment and Christly wisdom, yet I didn't touch on the nature of man's *communion* with Christ and the Almighty. It is one thing to develop discernment and scriptural wisdom and it is another to cultivate better patterns of communication with the Lord. There must be a healthy balance between personal individualism and collectivism in order for one to foster a spiritual relationship with his Creator. Too heavy of an emphasis on either component will cloud one's spiritual vision. It is also possible that one can strengthen and refine one's capacities for discernment and scriptural wisdom without actually refining one's spirit and connections with the Lord. If one does achieve a refinement of the soul without a refinement of the spirit, he will be highly susceptible to the modern scourge that is interpretational *structure building*. Discernment and wisdom can be used to buttress one's own position of theological authority without actually forging a deeper connection with the Almighty.

Make no mistake, personal individualism is still deeply intertwined with the development and nourishment of one's spirit. Fellowship and covenant between believers are extremely important forms of spiritual fulfillment, yet they mean nothing if the individuals involved lack the requisite *personal relationship* with Christ Jesus. It is highly important to mention this—a believer can have a personal relationship with Christ and *lack* communion and covenant with his brothers and sisters. A believer can also have communion and covenant *without* having a personal relationship with Jesus (although this is much harder). There is a dependency between these two things that we cannot overlook. We can look to 1 Corinthians 12 to see the gravity of this dependency between the man-to-God and man-to-man:

One Body but Many Parts

[12] There is one body, but it has many parts. But all its many parts make up one body. It is the same with Christ. [13] We were all baptized by one Holy Spirit. And so we are formed into one body. It didn't matter whether we were Jews or Gentiles, slaves or free people. We were all given the same Spirit to drink. [14] So the body is not made up of just one part. It has many parts.

[15] Suppose the foot says, "I am not a hand. So I don't belong to the body." By saying this, it cannot stop being part of the body. [16] And suppose the ear says, "I am not an eye. So I don't belong to the body." By saying this, it cannot stop being part of the body. [17] If the whole body were an eye, how could it hear? If the whole body were an ear, how could it smell? [18] God has placed each part in the body just as he wanted it to be. [19] If all the parts were the same, how could there be a body? [20] As it is, there are many parts. But there is only one body.

The gist of this: membership in the Body of Christ will signal a ripe personal relationship with the Lord, and a ripe personal relationship with Him will invite one into the Body of Christ. This is God's ideal dependency, and it is a sad fact that it does not exist in this form in modern society.

Perhaps the most plausible reason for the absence of this dependency is that modernity has placed a warped emphasis upon *societal* individualism. Where collectivism is pushed to the margins of society, man has little choice but to buttress his self-esteem and feed his material appetites. Personal individualism is used to strengthen the soul at the expense of the spirit. And once souls are strengthened in such a manner *en masse*, collectivism of all varieties grows increasingly harder to achieve. This is a "positive feedback loop" of self-righteousness and a "negative feedback loop" of selflessness.[8]

---

8. "Positive feedback" and "negative feedback" are technical terms used in diverse academic fields, from psychology to computer engineering. A system with positive feedback is one that has the following dynamic—X produces Y and Y produces *more* X. An example of positive feedback can be found in the stock market, where it is sometimes the case that the mass selling of stocks (X) causes a dip in stock price (Y) which then leads to mass buying and, ultimately, to more mass selling (X). Negative feedback is just the opposite of positive feedback, in which X produces Y and Y *decreases* X.

PART V: GETTING OFF THE COUCH AND INTO THE SPIRITUAL HOUSE

COLLECTIVISM & SOUL

Let's start out by reiterating something I mentioned in the "Individualism & Collectivism" subchapter:

> We must resist placing undue emphasis on the organization of society and economy, neglecting the role of the individual man and his spiritual growth and transformation. I think that the history of society is largely the history of the *overstatement* of man's external conditions, at the expense of his inner life and progression.

I think that the first and foremost reason why collectivism is considered taboo is because of these very tendencies.

Christly collectivism does not seek a solution from the outside in; it seeks a unification from the inside out. In other words, perhaps the biggest reason why modern collectivism has been so far removed from Christly collectivism is that the importance of a solid *personal individualism* has been neglected.

One parallel we can draw with this situation is that of the necessity of a well-educated, critically thinking electorate in democratic society. Thomas Jefferson himself said the following about this:

> If a nation expects to be ignorant and free, in a state of civilization, it expects what never was and never will be. [. . .] whenever the people are well-informed, they can be trusted with their own government; that, whenever things get so far wrong as to attract their notice, they may be relied on to set them right.[9]

The translation of this into terms of the spiritual house is this—we cannot expect to have a sturdy foundation and house without a sufficient strength of material of the individual stones. Alas, it is easy to misinterpret this point. From the prosperity gospel slant, the strength of the stones lies in their literal, *physical* qualities, from health to material wealth. These characteristics of man are *visible markers*; they are impossible to fully ignore. And it is for this reason that the prosperity gospel has been so wildly successful in the modern age.

What truly needs to be strengthened is each believer's spiritual self-awareness and connection to the Almighty. The *soul* simply serves as the *facilitator* of spiritual progress and *evaluator* of spiritual consumption. We

---

9. See McNergney and McNergney, *Education*, 75.

What Can Be Done?

can no longer hold out hope that our modern styles of worship—many of which are filled with showy and sexy spiritual junk food—will be able to unify us in Christ. We must look back to ancient ages and observe the gravity of the man-to-man covenant. We must grok the importance of communally-centered, grassroots worship. A genuine and fellowship-filled prayer group of ten of God's children holds more spiritual weight than an individualism-fueled, hundred-person church.

COLLECTIVISM & SPIRIT

Many people are familiar with the so-called "Jesus movement" of the sixties and seventies. This phenomenon brought countless young folks to Christ and swept the country with fiery fervor. The Jesus movement was the closest thing believers have seen to a communal revolution since the ancient days, and many aspects of it are instructional for the modern church.[10] At the same time, there is much to learn from the movement in terms of how *not* to go about a communal unification in Christ. Although former participants of the movement would vehemently disagree with this statement, it seems that the movement had an undercurrent of *structure building*—the branding and authoritative dissemination of "definitive" scriptural interpretation.

In 2 Peter 1:19–21 we see a spellbindingly applicable exhortation against such structure building:

> 19 And we have the prophetic word [about Jesus] more fully confirmed, to which you will do well to pay attention as to a lamp shining in a dark place, until the day dawns and the morning star rises in your hearts, 20 knowing this first of all, that no prophecy of Scripture comes from someone's own interpretation. 21 For no prophecy was ever produced by the will of man, but men spoke from God as they were carried along by the Holy Spirit.[11]

No prophecy of Scripture comes from someone's own interpretation.
No prophecy was ever produced by the will of man.
All of this underscores what I have said about the spiritual house in Christ—the structure itself is above and beyond the stones' composition

---

10. For an overview, see Bustraan, *The Jesus People Movement.*
11. ESV.

PART V: Getting off the Couch and into the Spiritual House

and position. The holy priesthood is an emergent and dynamic structure. We should expect no less from our wonderful Savior and his Father.

We cannot hope to blithely return to an ancient collectivism, suppressing our modern environment and state of affairs. We must toe the line between a luddite-like disdain for our world and an unbridled, hedonistic love for it. We must bring believers together *authentically* and *pragmatically*. If we can revive the ancient reverence for life and the gracious acceptance of demise, if we can restore the ancient practice of covenant and the steadfast love for one's neighbor, we will be well on our way to tapping into our spiritual roots in Christ, for Christ.

Bibliography

"Abortion." (n.d.). https://news.gallup.com/poll/1576/abortion.aspx.
Baggini, Julian. "What Is This Foolish Lust for Uncertainty?" *The Guardian* (October 2011). https://www.theguardian.com/commentisfree/belief/2011/oct/28/lust-for-uncertainty.
Balmer, Randall Herbert. *Encyclopedia of Evangelicalism*. Waco, TX: Baylor University Press, 2004.
Bearak, Max. "Climbing to Ethiopia's Church in the Sky." *The Washington Post* (December 2019).https://www.washingtonpost.com/graphics/2019/world/amp-stories/ethiopias-church-in-the-sky/.
Bemmelen, Peter van. "The Everlasting Covenant." *Journal of the Adventist Theological Society* 24 (2013) 92–106. https://digitalcommons.andrews.edu/cgi/viewcontent.cgi?article=1088&context=jats.
Bickel, Bruce, and Stan Jantz. *I'm Fine with God... It's Christians I Can't Stand: Getting Past the Religious Garbage in the Search for Spiritual Truth*. Eugene, OR: Harvest House, 2008.
Bookchin, Murray. *Social Ecology and Communalism*. Edinburgh, UK: AK, 2007.
Bowler, Kate. *Blessed: A History of the American Prosperity Gospel*. New York: Oxford University Press, 2018.
———. "Blessed: A History of the American Prosperity Gospel." PhD diss., Duke University, 2010.
Brown, Michael L. *Authentic Fire: A Response to John MacArthur's Strange Fire*. Lake Mary, FL: Creation House, 2015.
Brymer, Eric, and Robert D. Schweitzer. "Phenomenology and Extreme Sports in Natural Landscapes." In *Landscapes of Leisure: Space, Place and Identities*, 135–146. London, UK: Palgrave Macmillan, 2015.
Bustraan, Richard A. *The Jesus People Movement: A Story of Spiritual Revolution Among the Hippies*. Eugene, OR: Wipf & Stock, 2014.
"Changing Denominations Common Among Evangelical Leaders." (May 2015). https://www.nae.net/changing-denominations-common-among-evangelical-leaders/.
"Communalism." (n.d.). https://en.wikipedia.org/wiki/Communalism.
Copeland, Kenneth. "18 Bible Verses About Wealth and Prosperity." (n.d.). https://www.kcm.org/real-help/finances/apply/18-bible-verses-about-wealth-and-prosperity.
———. *Prosperity, the Choice is Yours*. Fort Worth, TX: KCP, 1985.
Crockett, Clayton. *Secular Theology: American Radical Theological Thought*. London, UK: Routledge, 2001.

Bibliography

Csikszent, Mihaly. *Flow.* New York: HarperCollins, 1991.
Curtin, Melanie. "In an 8-Hour Day, the Average Worker Is Productive for This Many Hours." *Inc.* (July 2016). https://www.inc.com/melanie-curtin/in-an-8-hour-day-the-average-worker-is-productive-for-this-many-hours.html.
Dawkins, Richard. *The Blind Watchmaker: Why the Evidence of Evolution Reveals a Universe Without Design.* New York: Norton, 1996.
Dillon, Michele, and Sarah Savage. "Values and Religion in Rural America: Attitudes Toward Abortion and Same-Sex Relations." *The Carsey School of Public Policy at the Scholars' Repository* 12 (2006) 1–10. https://scholars.unh.edu/carsey/12/.
Doig, Will, and Jennifer Ludden. "Cities—But Not Their Citizens—Really Are Meaner." *NPR* on *KERA* (April 2012). https://www.npr.org/2012/04/12/150507018/cities.
Drucker, Peter F. "The Age of Social Transformation." *The Atlantic Monthly* (November 1994). https://www.theatlantic.com/past/docs/issues/95dec/chilearn/drucker.htm.
Ellul, Jacques. *The Meaning of the City.* Eugene, OR: Wipf & Stock, 2011.
———. *Prayer and Modern Man.* Eugene, OR: Wipf & Stock, 2012.
———. *The Technological Society.* New York: Vintage, 1964.
Frobenius, Leo. *Kulturgeschichte Afrikas: Prolegomena zu einer historischen Gestaltlehre.* Wuppertal, DE: Hammer, 1998.
Gallup. "Abortion." (September 2020). https://news.gallup.com/poll/1576/abortion.aspx.
Gebser, Jean. *The Ever-Present Origin.* Athens, OH: Ohio University Press, 1997.
"Global Christianity – A Report on the Size and Distribution of the World's Christian Population." (December 2011). https://www.pewforum.org/2011/12/19/global-christianity-exec/.
Graham, Billy. "Don't Wait, Turn to Christ Today." (January 2017). https://www.bgdailynews.com/community/billy-graham-don-t-wait-turn-to-christ-today/article_b08103d3-14ff-59b7-9259-2d1c93113982.html.
Granberg-Michaelson, Wesley. "The Heresy of Individualism." (April 2020). https://www.thebanner.org/features/2020/04/the-heresy-of-individualism.
Hagin, Kenneth. *Zoe: The God-Kind of Life.* Garland, TX: K. Hagin Ministries, 1981.
Harvey, Graham, and Robert J. Wallis. *Historical Dictionary of Shamanism.* Lanham, MD: Rowman & Littlefield, 2015.
"Healing in Action: A Toolkit for Black Lives Matter Healing Justice & Direct Action." (n.d.). https://blacklivesmatter.com/wp-content/uploads/2018/01/BLM_HealingAction_r1.pdf.
Helwig, Alexa. "Teacher Sparks Controversy After Hanging BLM, Rainbow Flags in Virtual Classroom." *Local* 12 (September 2020). https://local12.com/news/local/teacher-sparks-controversy-after-hanging-blm-rainbow-flags-in-virtual-classroom-cincinnati.
Horton, Michael Scott. *Justification* (Vol. 1). Grand Rapids, MI: Zondervan, 2018.
"How Americans Spend Their Time." (n.d.). https://graphics.wsj.com/time-use/.
"Human Evolution Timeline Interactive." (October 2020). https://humanorigins.si.edu/evidence/human-evolution-timeline-interactive.
James, William. *Pragmatism and Other Writings.* New York: Penguin, 2000.
Jami, Criss. *Healology.* CreateSpace Independent, 2016.
Kant, Immanuel. *Groundwork for the Metaphysics of Morals.* Binghamton, NY: Yale University Press, 2008.

BIBLIOGRAPHY

Larson, Brad. "How Self-Help Can Become Self-Hurt." (July 2016). https://www.thegospelcoalition.org/article/how-self-help-can-become-self-hurt/.

Lebron, Christopher J. *The Making of Black Lives Matter: A Brief History of an Idea.* New York: Oxford University Press, 2017.

Lewis, C.S. *Mere Christianity.* In *The Complete C.S. Lewis Signature Classics*, 5–115. New York: HarperCollins, 2002.

———. *The Problem of Pain.* New York: HarperOne, 2001.

Light, Joe. "Leisure Trumps Learning in Time-Use Survey." *The Wall Street Journal* (June 2011). https://www.wsj.com/articles/SB10001424052702304657804576401890078537246.

Low, Keath. "The Relationship Between ADHD and Chronic Procrastination." *Verywell Mind* (August 2020). https://www.verywellmind.com/adhd-and-chronic-procrastination-20379.

Luft, Sebastian. *Subjectivity and Lifeworld in Transcendental Phenomenology.* Evanston, IL: Northwestern University Press, 2011.

MacArthur, John. *Strange Fire: The Danger of Offending the Holy Spirit with Counterfeit Worship.* Nashville, Tenneessee: Thomas Nelson, 2013.

Machiavelli, Niccolò. *Machiavelli: The Prince.* Cambridge, UK: Cambridge University Press, 2019.

McNeil, Ian. *An Encyclopedia of the History of Technology.* London, UK: Routledge, 2003.

McNergney, Robert F., and Joanne M. McNergney. *Education: The Practice and Profession of Teaching.* Boston, MA: Pearson, 2008.

Mize, Jonathan J., and Vincent Geilenberg. "Panentheism and the Problem of World Inclusion: A Category-Theoretic Approach." (March 2021). Forthcoming in *Philosophia*. https://www.researchgate.net/publication/349772775_Panentheism_and_the_Problem_of_World_Inclusion_A_Category-_Theoretic_Approach.

Mohrhoff, Ulrich. "Evolution of Consciousness According to Jean Gebser." *Anti-Matters* (2008). https://antimatters2.files.wordpress.com/2018/04/2-3-05-gebser-origin.pdf.

Needleman, Jacob, and John Piazza. *The Essential Marcus Aurelius.* New York: Penguin, 2008.

Neubauer, Hublin, et al. "The Evolution of Modern Human Brain Shape." *Science Advances* 4 (2018). https://advances.sciencemag.org/content/4/1/eaao5961.

Ostrom, Elinor. *Governing the Commons: The Evolution of Institutions of Collective Action.* Cambridge, UK: Cambridge University Press, 2015.

Padover, Saul K. *Thomas Jefferson on Democracy.* New York: New American Library, 1946.

Parker, Jared T. "Cutting Covenants." In *The Gospel of Jesus Christ in the Old Testament*, 109–28. Provo, UT: Brigham Young University Press, 2009.

Peale, Norman Vincent. *The Power of Positive Thinking.* Indirapuram, UP: Samaira, 2019.

Percy, Walker. *Lost in the Cosmos: The Last Self-Help Book.* New York: Picador USA, 2000.

Piper, John. *Don't Waste Your Life.* Wheaton, IL: Crossway, 2018.

Platt, David. *Radical: Taking Back Your Faith from the American Dream.* Colorado Springs: Multnomah, 2010.

Popper, Karl Raimund. *The Open Society and Its Enemies.* Princeton, NJ: Princeton University Press, 2013.

Ramberg, B. "Richard Rorty." (June 2007). https://plato.stanford.edu/entries/rorty/.

"Refrigerators Through the Decades." (August 2016). https://bigchill.com/us/blog/refrigerators-through-the-decades/.

Bibliography

"Religion." (n.d.). https://news.gallup.com/poll/1690/religion.aspx.

Robertson, Donald. *How to Think Like a Roman Emperor: The Stoic Philosophy of Marcus Aurelius*. New York: St. Martin's, 2019.

Schor, Juliet. *The Overworked American: The Unexpected Decline Of Leisure*. New York: Basic, 2008.

"Secular Theology." (n.d.). https://en.wikipedia.org/wiki/Secular_theology.

"Self-Centered Theology." (n.d.). https://www.fourthyearministries.com/2015/08/self-centered-theology.html.

Sincero, Jen. *You Are a Badass: How to Stop Doubting Your Greatness and Start Living an Awesome Life*. Philadelphia, PA: Running, 2017.

Stewart, Melville Y. *Science and Religion in Dialogue: Has Science Really Destroyed Its Own Religious Roots?* Malden, MA: Wiley-Blackwell, 2010.

"Technology Timeline (1752-1990)." https://www.pbs.org/wgbh/americanexperience/features/telephone-technology-timeline/.

Thomas, Deja, and Juliana Menasce Horowitz. "Support for Black Lives Matter Has Decreased Since June but Remains Strong Among Black Americans." *Pew Research Center* (September 2020). https://www.pewresearch.org/fact-tank/2020/09/16/support-for-black-lives-matter-has-decreased-since-june-but-remains-strong-among-black-americans/.

Tyldesley, Joyce. *Tutankhamen: The Search for an Egyptian King*. New York: Basic, 2012.

Um, Stephen T. *1 Corinthians: The Word of the Cross (Preaching the Word)*. Wheaton, IL: Crossway, 2015.

"Victoria Osteen | Do Good for your own self, Not for God | Billy Madison." (August 2014). https://www.youtube.com/watch?v=7RcIqhcNNhw.

Wehner, Peter. "The Deepening Crisis in Evangelical Christianity." *The Atlantic* (July 2019). https://www.theatlantic.com/ideas/archive/2019/07/evangelical-christians-face-deepening-crisis/593353/.

"Why Wicked CEOs Prevail: Dark Personality Traits of the Executive Suit." (November 2019). https://www2.monash.edu/impact/articles/management/why-wicked-ceos-prevail-dark-personality-traits-of-the-executive-suite/.

Wooden, Cindy. "Pope Calls for Politics to Rediscover Its Vocation to Work for Common Good." *Catholic News Service* (October 2020). https://www.catholicnews.com/pope-calls-for-politics-to-rediscover-its-vocation-to-work-for-common-good/.

Wright, N.T. *For All God's Worth: True Worship and the Calling of the Church*. Grand Rapids, MI: Eerdmans, 2014.

www.ingramcontent.com/pod-product-compliance
Lightning Source LLC
Chambersburg PA
CBHW072136160426
43197CB00012B/2125